Is Man the Measure?

Is Man the

Measure?

An Evaluation of Contemporary Humanism

Norman L. Geisler

BAKER BOOK HOUSE
Grand Rapids, Michigan 49506

Copyright 1983 by
Baker Book House Company

ISBN: 0-8010-3787-5

Library of Congress
Catalog Card Number: 82-84752

PHOTOLITHOPRINTED BY CUSHING - MALLOY, INC.
ANN ARBOR, MICHIGAN, UNITED STATES OF AMERICA

Contents

Preface

The term *humanism* is very much like the word *religion*. Both terms encompass a diverse patchwork of beliefs which have some common threads. There are, for example, many different religions—Buddhism, Christianity, Hinduism, Islam, and Judaism, to name a few—and within each of these there are differing points of view; for example, in Christianity there are differences between Roman Catholics, Greek Catholics, Episcopalians, Presbyterians, Lutherans, Methodists, Baptists, and other denominations.

Humanism, too, encompasses widely differing beliefs which have some elements in common with each other. There are evolutionary (chap. 1), behavioral (chap. 2), and existential humanists (chap. 3); we even find pragmatic (chap. 4), Marxist (chap. 5), egocentric (chap. 6), cultural (chap. 7), and Christian (chap. 8) forms of humanism. By examining each of these kinds of humanism two main goals can be accomplished. First, we can gain an insight into their distinctive differences and intramural conflicts. Second, a consensus of basic humanistic beliefs will emerge as we view the different varieties of humanism. This loosely defined coalition is what is popularly known as secular humanism. It is this humanistic consensus which most radically conflicts with Christian beliefs. Part Two will examine and evaluate secular humanism more carefully.

Not everything about humanism is bad from a Christian point of view. Indeed, there are many emphases within humanism which are compatible with Christian beliefs (see chaps. 8 – 9). On the other hand, secular humanism presents one of the greatest threats to the survival of Christianity in the world today. It is for this reason that a Christian should carefully study its basic beliefs and scrutinize their adequacy. As one does this, however, it should be kept in mind that the right to critique another view must be earned. One should not criticize another position until he has understood it and learned something from it. Only then does one have the right to reject it. It is for this reason that Part One is largely expository; systematic evaluation is found mainly in the second part of the book. All too often evaluations jump to critical conclusions with too little understanding and appreciation of the view being evaluated. It is, therefore, my hope that the reader will study carefully the expositions in the first half of this book before he reads the evaluations in the second half.

I am grateful to William Watkins for his able assistance in the preparation of this book.

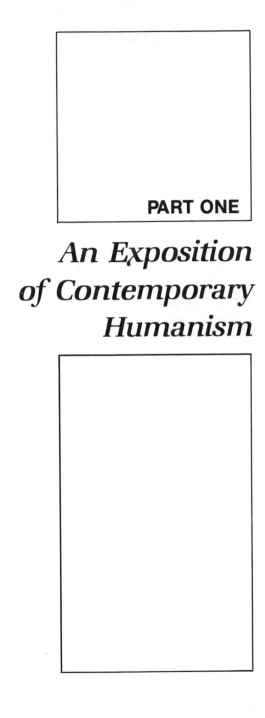

PART ONE

An Exposition of Contemporary Humanism

1

Evolutionary Humanism

One of the most influential forms of modern humanism is evolutionary humanism. It was given its most complete expression in Julian Huxley's famous book *Religion Without Revelation*. Building on the evolutionary biology of Charles Darwin, the evolutionary philosophy of Herbert Spencer, and the evolutionary ethics of his grandfather, Thomas H. Huxley, Julian developed a complete evolutionary humanism. He expressed views on a whole gamut of topics including God, human origins, religion, values, science, the arts, and his hopes for the future possibilities of the race.

God and Religion

Huxley's Disbelief in God

Huxley was strongly opposed to any belief in God but in favor of religion. He believed that we quite assuredly at present know nothing beyond this world and natural experience. That is, "a personal God, be he Jehovah, or Allah, or Apollo, or Amen-Ra, or without name but simply God, I know nothing of." Furthermore, "I am not merely agnostic on the subject.... I disbelieve in a personal God in any sense in which that phrase is ordinarily used."[1]

The basis for belief in God, Huxley held, is purely psychological. "As I see it broadly, 'God the Father' is a personification of the forces of non-human nature; 'God the Holy Ghost' represents all ideals; and

---

1. Julian Huxley, *Religion Without Revelation* (New York: Mentor, 1957), pp. 17 – 18.

'God the Son' personifies human nature at its highest." Thus the gods are creations of man, personalized representations of the forces of destiny, the projection of human thought and imagination.[2]

Huxley believed that as a result of modern scientific understanding the concept of God was becoming obsolete. He wrote that "God can no longer be considered as the controller of the universe in any but a pickwickian sense. The god hypothesis is no longer of any pragmatic value." As far as having any effect on the world is concerned, "God is beginning to resemble not a ruler, but the last fading smile of a cosmic Cheshire Cat."[3] In fact, Huxley believed that it would soon be as impossible for an intelligent person to believe in a god as it is now to believe that the earth is flat.[4]

Huxley's disbelief in God brought him great relief. "For my own part," he concluded, "the sense of spiritual relief which comes from rejecting the idea of God as a supernatural being is enormous." He passionately hoped others would join him in his belief (and relief); for if they would, the insufferable arrogance of those who claim to be in sole possession of religious truth would happily disappear. Along with this would go bigotry, religious war, religious persecution, the horrors of the Inquisition, and attempts to suppress knowledge and learning; social and moral change would quickly take place upon the removal of these evils.[5]

Huxley's Belief in Religion

Despite his strong disbelief in God, Huxley was a deeply religious person. Why? "I believe," said Huxley, "that it is necessary to believe something. Complete scepticism does not work."[6] But one cannot believe just anything. "The method which has proved effective, as a matter of actual fact, in providing a firm foundation for belief ... is usually called the scientific method." So Huxley believed that the scientific method is the only method which in the long run will provide a satisfactory foundation for beliefs.[7]

When Huxley applied the scientific method to religious experi-

2. Ibid., p. 51.
3. Ibid., pp. 58 – 59.
4. Ibid., p. 62.
5. Ibid., p. 32.
6. Ibid., p. 13.
7. Ibid., p. 15.

ences, he concluded, as did Rudolf Otto, that "religion arose as a feeling of the sacred." Huxley believed that experiencing this feeling is a fundamental capacity of man, something given in and by the construction of human nature.[8]

Huxley spoke honestly and vividly of his own religious experiences:

> Another incident of the same year remains vividly with me. We were doing night exercises between Aldershot and Fleet: the warm June night was scented with broom: the monotony of exercise, enforced silence, and darkness, combined with the beauty of the hour, impelled to aimless meditation.
>
> Suddenly, for no particular reason, without apparent connection with other thoughts, a problem and its solution flashed across my mind. I had understood how it was that two views or courses of action could not only both be sincerely held as good, but both actually could *be* good—and when the two came into contact, the one could both appear and be evil. It can be so when both are aiming in the same general direction, but the one is moving so much more slowly that it becomes a drag on the other's wheel.
>
> Ideas and facts, particular examples and their general meaning, the tragedy of bitter conflict between two fine realities, two solid honesties, all jostled each other in my mind in that moment of insight, and I had made a new step towards that peaceful basis for action which is expressed by the French proverb, *"Tout comprendre, c'est tout pardonner."*
>
> It also had that definite quality of being thrown into consciousness, implied in the term revelation, which has been described for purely intellectual discovery by many mathematicians and men of science, notably Poincaré in his essays on scientific method. It was an exaggeration of the sense that comes when one suddenly sees a point which had eluded comprehension, but without any accompanying sense of effort. The same general sense in the sphere of feeling one may have when one is suddenly transported to a complete peace and satisfaction by some sudden view of distant hills over plain; or by a sudden quality of light—"the light that never was on sea or land," and yet is suddenly here, transforming a familiar landscape; or by a poem or a picture, or a face. But only once before had I had such a complete sense of outside givenness in an experience—the only occasion on which I had had a vision (of a non-hallucinatory but amazingly real sort: such, of a religious cast, abound in the records of mystics such as St. Theresa).[9]

8. Ibid., p. 21.
9. Ibid., pp. 86 – 87.

Such vivid religious experiences left Huxley with passionate "beliefs in the supreme value of certain ideas and activities." He noted that in theological parlance such beliefs are called faith.[10] In fact, Huxley frankly confessed, "Life would have been intolerable but for [such] glimpses of the alternative state, occasional moments of great happiness and spiritual refreshment, coming usually through poetry or through beautiful landscape, or through people."[11]

One day while browsing through a library in Colorado Springs Huxley came across some essays by Lord Morley in which he found these words: "The next great task of science will be to create a religion for humanity." Huxley was challenged by this vision. He wrote, "I was fired by sharing his conviction that science would of necessity play an essential part in framing any religion of the future worthy of the name."[12]

Man and Moral Duty

Huxley took up Morley's challenge to develop a scientific religion. He called it evolutionary humanism. One of the foundational tenets, as the name signifies, is the theory of evolution.

The Evolution of Man

The experience of the mystical led Huxley to reject a purely materialistic interpretation of the universe such as he saw in Marxism. He concluded, "The materialist hypothesis, in denying the importance of mental and spiritual factors in the cosmos, is to me as erroneous as, though more sophisticated than, the naive notion of the magic hypothesis, which projects spiritual forces into material events." His rejection of pure materialism notwithstanding, Huxley was a complete naturalist. He insisted that "the discoveries of physiology, general biology, and psychology not only make possible, but necessitate, a naturalistic hypothesis, in which there is no room for the supernatural." Furthermore, he believed that the spiritual forces

10. Ibid., p. 76.
11. Ibid., p. 77.
12. Ibid., p. 82.

at work in the cosmos are just as much a part of nature as are the material forces.[13]

Evolution is of course a naturalistic explanation of the origin of life. Huxley wrote, "I personally believe in the uniformity of nature, in other words, that Nature is seen to be orderly." By this he meant that "there are not two realms of reality, one natural, the other supernatural and from time to time invading and altering the course of events in the natural."[14] Huxley believed not only in the unity of nature but also in unity by continuity. That is, matter does not appear or disappear, nor do living things arise except from previously existing things essentially like themselves. Hence "the more complex matter that is alive must at some time have originated from matter that was not alive."[15]

As evolution moved onward it moved upward. For we find that "each new dominant type possesses some improvement in general organization.... This progressive replacement of dominant types and groups is most clearly shown in the later history of vertebrates." It is thus perfectly proper, said Huxley, to use terms like *higher* and *lower* to describe different types of organism, and *progress* for certain types of trend.[16]

The culmination of the evolutionary biological process is man. Therefore Huxley believed that "the only avenue of major advance left open was through the improvement of brain and mind." Furthermore, it was clear to Huxley that "man is only at the beginning of his period of evolutionary dominance, and that vast and still undreamt-of possibilities of further advance still be before him."[17]

Biology has revealed man's destiny. Man "is the highest form of life produced by the evolutionary process on this planet, the latest dominant type, and the only organism capable of further major advance or progress." In other words, his destiny is to realize new possibilities for the whole world and to be the instrument of further evolutionary process on this planet.[18]

13. Ibid., p. 187.
14. Ibid., p. 45.
15. Ibid.
16. Ibid., p. 192.
17. Ibid., p. 193.
18. Ibid.

The Nature of Man

Huxley was not a wide-eyed optimist about the nature of man. He believed that "there is evil in man as well as good."[19] He recognized man's evil urges and activities such as greed, arrogance, fanaticism, sadism, and self-indulgence.[20] He believed, however, that man is capable of saving himself from these evils.

Furthermore, Huxley was not a strict materialist. He believed that the stuff of the universe has "spiritual" and "mental" aspects as well as "material."[21] He rejected Marxist materialism and spoke favorably about "mystical" experience. He was nonetheless a committed naturalist in explaining the phenomenon of human existence.

One thing is clear, however: Huxley was optimistic about man's ability to achieve a great future. Man is the only hope for future evolution. Along with his grandfather T. H. Huxley, Julian confessed, "My faith is in the possibilities of man."[22] His hope was that man would continue to realize new potentialities through continued evolution.

Evolution and Ethics

The evolutionary progress of the past provides us with guiding principles for the future ("the past history of biological evolution gives us a certain future guidance"). On this basis we can extrapolate some of the main trends of progress into the future, and conclude that man should aim at a continued increase of those qualities which have spelled progress in the biological past. These guiding principles for the future include "efficiency and control of environment, self-regulation and independence of outer changes, individuation and level of organization, wholeness or harmony of working, extent of awareness and knowledge, storage of experience, and degree of mental organization."[23] In particular, said Huxley, man is more likely to achieve his destiny if he exploits fully those improvements which have given him his position as latest dominant type, such as the properties of reason, imagination, and conceptual thought, and his

19. Ibid., p. 196.
20. Ibid., p. 197.
21. Ibid., pp. 186 – 187.
22. Ibid., p. 212.
23. Ibid., p. 193.

unique capacities of accumulating, organizing, and applying experience through a transmissible culture.[24]

One of man's unique abilities is to construct religion. "Man's most sacred duty, and at the same time his most glorious opportunity, is to promote the maximum fulfillment of the evolutionary process on this earth; and this includes the fullest realization of his own inherent possibilities."[25] But even though Huxley sees the flowering of the individual as having intrinsic value, as being an end in itself, nonetheless the primacy of the individual is not absolute. Rather, it is limited by the need of maintaining and improving social organization.[26] For the duties the individual has toward his own potentialities he owes also to others, singly and collectively. That is, "he has the duty to aid other individuals towards fuller development, and to contribute his mite to the maintenance and improvement of the continuing social process, and so to the march of evolution as a whole."[27]

According to Huxley the basic postulate of evolutionary humanism is that mental and spiritual forces do have operative effect, and "are indeed of decisive importance in the highly practical business of working out human destiny; and that they are not supernatural, not outside man but within him."[28] These forces operate not only within man but also through the social process. Since man is the only one in conscious control of these forces, he alone is responsible for realizing life's further progress. Man's responsibility to be in control applies, said Huxley, as much to the blind urge to reproduction as it does to personal greed or desire for power, as much to arrogance and fanaticism as to straightforward sadism or self-indulgence.[29]

In general, evolutionary humanism views the duty of the individual as the optimum realization of his possibilities. More specifically, this involves two things. First, "the right kind of individual development is ... one which leaves the way permanently open for fresh possibilities of growth." Second, there are three areas of personal development possible: "one is specialization. ... The second we may call allroundness by summation: the cultivation of every kind of ful-

24. Ibid.
25. Ibid., p. 194.
26. Ibid., pp. 194 – 195.
27. Ibid., p. 195.
28. Ibid.
29. Ibid., p. 197.

fillment separately.... The third...we may call comprehensive wholeness: the cultivation of inner harmony and peace."[30]

Actually evolutionary humanism has twin goals: present personal fulfillment and long-term cosmic progress. The latter value Huxley calls "the gospel of evolutionary humanism," which he sees as a "transcendent value."[31] Thus the conclusions dictated by evolutionary humanism can be briefly summed up as follows. "First, man finds one of his ultimate fulfillments in comprehension.... Secondly, accumulated and organized knowledge and experience are necessary instruments or organs for human advance."[32]

Science and the Future

Although Huxley did not believe in individual immortality, whether in heaven or hell,[33] he did expect the human race to continue. He believed that science is the best organ for accomplishing this goal— not science without religion, but a scientific religion:

> Twentieth-century man, it is clear, needs a new organ for dealing with destiny, a new system of religious beliefs and attitudes adapted to the new situation in which his societies now have to exist. The radically new feature of the present situation may perhaps be stated thus: Earlier religions and belief-systems were largely adaptations to cope with man's ignorance and fears, with the result that they came to concern themselves primarily with stability of attitude. But the need to-day is for a belief-system adapted to cope with his knowledge and his creative possibilities; and this implies the capacity to meet, inspire and guide change.[34]

Humanistic religion, then, is the organ of destiny. However, Huxley had no delusions of grandeur about the immediate success of this kind of religion. He felt that like all other new religions it would at first be expressed and spread by a small minority. However, he predicted that in due course of time it would become universal, not

30. Ibid., pp. 199 – 200.
31. Ibid., p. 201.
32. Ibid., p. 204.
33. Ibid., p. 18.
34. Ibid., p. 188.

only potentially and in theory, but actually and in practice. Why? Because, argued Huxley, the properties of man's psychological nature make this inevitable. Man cannot avoid the process of convergence which makes for the integration of divergent or hostile human groups in a single organic world society and culture.[35]

In short, there is an unavoidable evolutionary process which will eventuate in a universal humanistic religion. This atheistic society will continue the evolutionary development of man in ever-new intellectual, psychological, and social ways.

Precisely what form this new universal humanistic religion would take Huxley was unable to prognosticate. He confessed,

> How that religion will take form—what rituals or celebrations it might practise, whether it will equip itself with any sort of professional body or priesthood, what buildings it will erect, what symbols it will adopt—that is something which no one can prophesy.[36]

He was confident, however, that it would come and that since the scientific spirit and the scientific method have proved the most effective agents for the comprehension and control of physical nature, it simply remains for man to apply them to the comprehension and control of human destiny.[37]

An Evaluation of Evolutionary Humanism

Evolutionary humanism is much broader than Huxley's variety of it. In fact, virtually all humanists believe in some form of evolution. What they disagree about is not the fact of evolution but its mechanism. For instance, many evolutionists do not agree with Huxley's premise that natural selection (the survival of the fittest) is the means by which evolution is accomplished. There are two further distinguishing marks of Huxley's variety of evolutionary humanism. First, he believed it should be made a universal religion for all mankind and that such a religion is essential. Second, he believed that evo-

35. Ibid., p. 208.
36. Ibid., p. 209.
37. Ibid., p. 205.

lution is the basis for ethics. That is, whatever aids the evolutionary process is good and what hinders it is evil.

With almost a generation of hindsight several observations can be made on Huxley's vision. First, as a religion Huxley's dream has not caught on quickly. And it would seem that many secular humanists do not really desire it to catch on. Second, as later humanists admit (cf. "Humanist Manifesto II," 1973), the dreams of the early humanists, such as Huxley, were too optimistic. There is no good evidence to indicate the inevitability of the evolution of a universal humanistic religion. Third, the evolutionary ethic involves some serious problems. There is the problem of how to preserve the individual rights of those who are blocking social evolution. Also, there is the problem of deriving an ethical "ought" from a biological "is." That is, how can the assumed fact of evolution be the basis for moral value? Since many bad things as well as good evolve, there has to be some standard outside of the evolutionary process by which one can determine whether something is good or bad. Fourth, some will welcome Huxley's confession of "transcendent" and "supreme" values, "mystical" experience, and a "destiny" of the world as indicators of a surrogate "God." They will insist that only minds can "destine" and that only persons can be the object of religious commitments. They will contend that Huxley has avoided only the name *God* but not the reality. Finally, it seems reasonable to conclude that whatever other humanists may reject in Huxley's view, his evolutionism, naturalism, and skepticism about traditional religion will be universally applauded.[38]

38. See chaps. 10 – 15.

2

Behavioral Humanism

Some forms of humanism stress human freedom (e.g., existentialism). Others desire to go "beyond freedom and dignity" and emphasize that man is behaviorally determined. The most noted contemporary proponent of this view is the Harvard psychologist B. F. Skinner.

The background of Skinner's thought is found in *Behavior*, a book by J. B. Watson (d. 1958), an avowed atheist. In this book and subsequent works Watson launched an aggressive attack against the introspective method of psychology. He argued that because such things as consciousness and mind are unobservable and thus inaccessible to the observational and experimental methods of science, they are not proper objects of the study of psychology. On the other hand, since the behavior of all organisms is observable and therefore accessible to scientific inquiry, psychology, he proposed, should be the study of behavior. Thus a purely objective approach can be taken to the study of man.[1]

The essence of Skinner's radical behaviorism is that all organisms (indeed all that exists) are purely physical, the products solely of physical causes. This radical materialism shapes all of Skinner's thought. We will deal with its influence on Skinner more fully by examining his thought on the origin and nature of man, knowledge, ethics, will, God, religion, and the destiny of man.

1. Excellent summaries of Watson's thought can be found in J. D. Uytman, "Watson, John Broadus," in *The Encyclopedia of Philosophy*, ed. Paul Edwards (New York: Macmillan, 1967); and Leslie Stevenson, *Seven Theories of Human Nature* (New York: Oxford University, 1974), pp. 91 – 93.

Specific Beliefs of Behavioral Humanism

Man's Origin and Nature

Skinner holds that the origin of man can be accounted for by the theory of evolution. In fact he openly acknowledges his indebtedness to Darwin's evolutionary proposal and his "preoccupation with the continuity of species."[2] Skinner considers Darwin's work to have been the "entering wedge" that was needed "to show that man was not essentially different from the lower animals—that every human characteristic, including consciousness and reasoning powers, could be found in other species."[3] Darwin's theory of natural selection "explained the origination of millions of different species on the surface of the earth, without appealing to a creative mind."[4] Thus for the first time in the physical or biological sciences "the origin of a fantastic variety of living things could be explained by the contribution which novel features, possibly of random provenance, made to survival."[5] The origin of man was a "happy" accident of matter plus motion plus time plus chance plus natural selection. There was no "creative mind" behind the process, nor "inbuilt design" within it.

Building upon this view of the origin of man, Skinner develops his view of the nature of man. For him man is a purely "biological system." There is no nonphysical side of man, such as mind or consciousness. Skinner wholeheartedly rejects mentalistic phenomena such as these. He believes such ideas "almost certainly originated in primitive animism,"[6] a doctrine "which in its crudest form held that the body was moved by one or more indwelling spirits."[7] Materialistic views of man probably faded "because of a longstanding conviction that for much of human behavior there are no relevant antecedents."[8] We have desired to see man as one who "is a *center* from which behavior emanates," that is, as one who "initiates, originates, and

2. B. F. Skinner, "Behaviorism at Fifty," in *Contemporary Readings in Psychology,* ed. John M. Foley et al. (New York: Harper & Row, 1970), p. 17.

3. Ibid.

4. Skinner, *About Behaviorism* (New York: Alfred A. Knopf, 1974), p. 224.

5. Ibid., p. 36.

6. Skinner, "Behaviorism at Fifty," p. 16.

7. Skinner, *About Behaviorism,* p. 167.

8. Skinner, *Beyond Freedom and Dignity* (New York: Bantam, 1971), p. 11.

creates, and in doing so . . . remains, as he was for the Greeks, divine."[9] This is to view man as autonomous; that is to say, "his behavior is uncaused."[10]

Skinner believes that this view of man as autonomous is scientifically "vulnerable." He explains, "Autonomous man serves to explain only the things we are not yet able to explain in other ways. His existence depends upon our ignorance, and he naturally loses status as we come to know more about behavior."[11] In other words, Skinner has an unwavering faith in the ability of science to be able (one day) to fully demonstrate the physiological nature of all human behavior. Indeed, he believes that "the task of a scientific analysis is to explain how the behavior of a person as a physical system is related to the conditions under which the human species evolved and the conditions under which the individual lives." Hence Skinner cries out for the abolition of autonomous man, exclaiming that "his abolition has been long overdue."[12] In fact, since autonomous man is at the root of such global problems as overpopulation, mass starvation, and the ever-growing possibility of a nuclear holocaust, it is an absolute necessity that he be destroyed in order "to prevent the abolition of the human species."[13] Therefore, states Skinner, "To man *qua* man we readily say good riddance. Only by dispossessing him can we turn to the real causes of human behavior."[14] And in this way we can solve man's gravest problems.

In the place of the "prescientific" autonomous man Skinner gives us the "scientific" biological man. In this view "man *is* an animal, though a remarkable one."[15] He is as thoroughly physical as anything else that exists; the only difference is in the amazing complexity of his behavior. He is also "a member of a species shaped by evolutionary contingencies of survival, displaying behavioral processes which bring him under the control of the environment in which he lives."[16] In other words, his behavior is the result of heredity plus the envi-

9. Ibid., p. 12.
10. Ibid., p. 17.
11. Ibid., p. 12.
12. Ibid., p. 191.
13. Ibid.
14. Ibid.
15. Skinner, *About Behaviorism*, p. 239.
16. Skinner, *Beyond Freedom and Dignity*, pp. 201 – 202.

ronment and nothing more. The Skinnerian man is thus "a machine in the sense that he is a complex system behaving in lawful [and determined] ways, but the complexity is extraordinary."[17]

In short, the Skinnerian man is defined in terms of his behavior as purely physical and the product solely of physical causes. As Skinner puts it, "The more thoroughly we understand the relation between human behavior and its genetic and environmental antecedents, the more clearly we understand the nature or essence of the species."[18]

Man's Knowledge

It seems clear that if man is only a biological animal (Skinner even says that to compare man to a dog is a step forward from comparing him to a god![19]), then like other animals he must not have a mind (in the generally accepted sense of that term). With this Skinner heartily agrees. But he does not do what many scientists and philosophers have done, that is, identify the mind with the brain. He thinks that "both the mind and the brain are not far from the ancient notion of a homunculus—an inner person who behaves in precisely the ways necessary to explain the behavior of the outer person in whom he dwells."[20] Of course Skinner rejects the notion of an "inner man." Instead he proposes what he believes to be a "much simpler solution," that is, "to identify the mind with the person,"[21] which, of course, *is* his behavior. Skinner says,

> Human thought is human behavior. The history of human thought is what people have said and done. Mathematical symbols are the products of written and spoken verbal behavior, and the concepts and relationships of which they are symbols are in the environment. Thinking has the dimensions of behavior, not of a fancied inner process which finds expression in behavior.[22]

17. Ibid., p. 193.
18. Skinner, *About Behaviorism*, p. 226.
19. Skinner, *Beyond Freedom and Dignity*, p. 192.
20. Skinner, *About Behaviorism*, p. 117.
21. Ibid.
22. Ibid., pp. 117 – 118.

Now since "thinking is behaving,"[23] and since all behavior is the product of heredity plus the environment, it follows that thinking itself is a product of these elements. Consequently what man knows and the processes by which he comes to know are fully determined by nonrational processes and controls. Furthermore, Skinner adds, these nonrational causes are completely external to man. He does not take in and possess any of the real world, nor does he make copies of it so that he might store it in his memory for later retrieval.[24] Instead "the direction of the controlling relation is reversed: a person does not act upon the world, the world acts upon him."[25] And for Skinner, the world—that is, the environment—*"stays where it is and where it has always been—outside the body."*[26] The Skinnerian man, therefore, is a receiver and not a perceiver. He is passive, not active, in the knowing process. It is the environment, not man, which determines what man knows and how he will come to know it.

Skinner agrees that this applies to himself as well. Toward the end of the first chapter of his book *About Behaviorism*, Skinner writes, "I believe I have written a consistent, coherent account, but it reflects my own environmental history."[27] Hence all knowledge, Skinner's included, is the accidental product of nonrational physical causes acting upon and through purely physical organisms.

This view of human knowledge results in a pragmatic and relativistic concept of truth. For example, when discussing scientific knowledge as verbal behavior, Skinner says, "It [scientific knowledge] is a corpus of rules for effective action, and there is a special sense in which it could be 'true' if it yields the most effective action possible." In other words, "a proposition is 'true' to the extent that with its help the listener responds effectively to the situation it describes."[28] This is the same as saying that if a proposition, rule, command, or what-have-you works in a particular situation it must then be true. This is pragmatism. In Skinner's utopian novel, *Walden Two*, this pragmatic concept of truth is worked out in the community's code of conduct. The formulation of the "Walden Code" is approached in a completely "experimental way" by first consulting a great number

23. Ibid., p. 104.
24. Ibid., pp. 72 – 73.
25. Skinner, *Beyond Freedom and Dignity*, p. 202.
26. Skinner, *About Behaviorism*, p. 73.
27. Ibid., p. 18.
28. Ibid., p. 235.

of ethical works such as "Plato, Aristotle, Confucius, the New Testament, the Puritan divines, Machiavelli, Chesterfield, [and] Freud." Whatever is thought to be useful for "shaping human behavior" is adopted into the "Walden Code."[29] Hence truth is considered to be whatever works for the achievement of the desired end. In short, truth is what works.

Skinner also believes that truth is relative, not absolute. "The truth of a statement of fact is limited by the sources of the behavior of the speaker. . . . There is no way in which a verbal description of a setting can be absolutely true. . . . Again, there can be no absolute. No deduction from a rule or law can therefore be absolutely true. Absolute truth can be found, if at all, only in rules derived from rules, and here it is mere tautology."[30]

To summarize, Skinner identifies man's knowledge with his behavior, which is the product of nonrational external causes. And since such causes are continually subject to change, truth must also be subject to change and thus must always be defined as that which works.

Man's Ethics

In *About Behaviorism* Skinner poses the question, "Is a person moral because he behaves morally, or does he behave morally because he is moral?" His answer to this question is a resounding "neither." Says Skinner, a person "behaves morally *and* we call him moral because he lives in a particular kind of environment."[31] As he puts it elsewhere, "man has not evolved as an ethical or moral animal." Instead "he has evolved to the point at which he has constructed an ethical or moral culture"[32]; that is, "what has evolved is a social environment in which individuals behave in ways determined in part by their effects on others."[33] Hence man is not innately good or evil nor has he "an inborn need or demand for ethical standards."[34] Instead man is intrinsically nonmoral, the product of a nonmoral environment which in turn causes him to act in ways we call "moral."

29. Skinner, *Walden Two* (New York: Macmillan, 1976), p. 96.
30. Skinner, *About Behaviorism*, p. 136.
31. Ibid., p. 194.
32. Skinner, *Beyond Freedom and Dignity*, p. 167.
33. Skinner, *About Behaviorism*, p. 195.
34. Skinner, *Walden Two*, p. 182; cf. *Beyond Freedom and Dignity*, p. 167.

If man is essentially nonmoral, what then is the "good"? In Skinner's view the good, or rather those things we call good, are positive reinforcers, and those things we call bad or evil are negative reinforcers. Putting it plainly, he says, "Epicurus was not quite right: pleasure is not the ultimate good, pain the ultimate evil; the only good things are positive reinforcers, and the only bad things are negative reinforcers."[35] Skinner describes what he means by "reinforcing":

> When a bit of behavior has the kind of consequence called reinforcing, it is more likely to occur again. A positive reinforcer strengthens any behavior that produces it: a glass of water is positively reinforcing when we are thirsty, and if we then draw and drink a glass of water, we are more likely to do so again on similar occasions.[36]

Hence anything which makes reoccurrence of some behavior likely is called good. And anything which makes reoccurrence of behavior unlikely is called bad or evil.

One may ask, "But what determines what is good behavior and what is bad?" Skinner's answer is that whatever the members of one's culture find "reinforcing as the result of their genetic endowment and the natural and social contingencies to which they have been exposed" will be that culture's value system.[37] In brief, a person's culture determines what is right or wrong, good or bad; it makes such value judgments because it has been caused to do so by nonmoral physical causes, namely heredity and environment. Therefore the ultimate responsibility for an individual's or culture's moral code or even moral behavior lies not with the individual nor with the culture but with the environment. As Skinner clearly states, "We shall not solve the problems of alcoholism and juvenile delinquency by increasing a sense of responsibility. It is the environment which is 'responsible' for the objectional behavior, and it is the environment, not some attribute of the individual, which must be changed."[38] Therefore, since "all control is exerted by the environment," if we want people to be better "morally" we must "proceed to the design of better environments."[39]

35. Skinner, *Beyond Freedom and Dignity*, p. 102.
36. Skinner, *About Behaviorism*, p. 46.
37. Skinner, *Beyond Freedom and Dignity*, p. 122.
38. Ibid., p. 70.
39. Ibid., p. 77.

Man's Will

From all that has been said it should be clear that Skinnerian man is not free. Instead he is absolutely determined by physical causes to be what he is. Skinner is adamant on this point: "A scientific analysis of behavior must, I believe, assume that a person's behavior is controlled by his genetic and environmental histories rather than by the person himself as an initiating, creative agent."[40] He reiterates, "A person is not an originating agent"—that is, his behavior is not uncaused—but "he is a locus, a point at which many genetic and environmental conditions come together in a joint effect."[41] To put it another way, man is an instrumental or secondary cause—he is like a knife in the hands of a butcher or a gun in the hands of a hunter. But unlike the butcher or the hunter (in the traditional view of man anyway), the causes which drive man are nonrational and purposeless.

Furthermore, Skinner's determinism rules out any possibility of freedom of choice. Whatever man chooses to do is determined by external causes. There is no possibility that any individual could have chosen a course of action other than the one he in fact did choose. However, this is not to say that individuals cannot or do not make choices of any kind. Skinner does not rule out choice, only the freedom of choice. For him, "to exercise a choice is simply to act, and the choice a person is capable of making is the act itself."[42] In other words, a person's act of choosing is simply the person's behavior. But every person's behavior is caused by heredity and environment. Hence every person's behavior is not free, but completely determined. There is, therefore, no freedom of choice, only determined choice.

Now Skinner is the first to admit that "we cannot prove ... that human behavior as a whole is fully determined,"[43] but he nevertheless believes that complete determinism should be assumed. Skinner's reasons for such an assumption are as follows:

First, the very "nature of scientific inquiry" favors determinism over free will.[44] Science functions on the premise that all events are gov-

---

40. Skinner, *About Behaviorism*, p. 189.
41. Ibid., p. 168; cf. "Behaviorism at Fifty," p. 17.
42. Skinner, *About Behaviorism*, p. 113.
43. Ibid., p. 189.
44. Skinner, *Beyond Freedom and Dignity*, p. 97.

erned by causal laws. And since human behavior is an event (or rather series of events), it must be governed by causal laws. Now anything governed by causal laws must be determined. Therefore human behavior must be determined. Thus Skinner concludes, "If we are to use the methods of science in the field of human affairs, we must assume that behavior is lawful and determined."[45]

Secondly, to be free means that a person's behavior is either uncaused or caused by an "inner man" within the skin, neither of which is acceptable:

1. Behavior is not uncaused. (a) Scientific analysis of man continues to demonstrate that what was once thought to be uncaused behavior is in fact caused by the environment.[46] (b) The view that behavior is uncaused is not as advantageous as determinism, for by definition uncaused behavior is unchangeable. This places man's behavior in the hands of chance or whim, making it impossible to change his behavior so as to solve our global problems.[47] (c) The view that behavior is uncaused and thus man has free will contradicts the behaviorist's view that man is determined. This final point is put well by Frazier, one of the characters in *Walden Two*: "I deny that freedom exists at all. I must deny it—or my program would be absurd. You can't have a science about a subject matter which hops capriciously about."[48]

2. A person's behavior is not caused by some "inner man" within the skin, for such mentalistic notions are mythical, being postulated to explain behavior which we cannot yet explain in another way.[49]

Therefore, concludes Skinner, man is not free. And if he is not free, then he must be completely determined, or at least we should assume as much.

Now since man is fully determined, we must conclude that "little or nothing remains for autonomous man to do and receive credit for doing." For if he is fully determined, man "does not engage in moral struggle and therefore has no chance to be a moral hero or credited with inner virtues."[50] Hence man cannot be credited or blamed for anything he does. Instead the credit and blame must be shifted to

45. Quoted from Stevenson, *Seven Theories of Human Nature*, p. 97.
46. Skinner, *Beyond Freedom and Dignity*, pp. 17 – 19, 96.
47. Ibid., pp. 96, 204 – 205.
48. Skinner, *Walden Two*, pp. 241 – 242.
49. Skinner, *Beyond Freedom and Dignity*, p. 12.
50. Ibid., p. 76.

the environment, for whatever man does he does because the environment has caused him to do it.[51] Skinner drives this point home by contending that Adolf Hitler's program of genocide "was caused by environmental events in Hitler's personal history."[52] It was the environment that caused Hitler to order the extermination of over six million Jews. Thus Hitler should not be held responsible for his actions. It is the environment we should blame. And if "we want to do anything about genocide" in the future "it is to the environment we must turn."[53] Change the environment in the right way, and we can prevent the occurrence of another genocide.

In summary, Skinner's view of the will of man is that man is fully determined by external causes which are fully responsible for his behavior. To change man's behavior one must change man's environment—nothing else will do.

Man's God(s) and Religions

During an interview on William F. Buckley's television show, "Firing Line," Skinner said that he was "in no position to pronounce any judgment on the existence or non-existence of God."[54] However, during the same interview he was willing to state his position on the origin of belief in God. Said Skinner, "I think men have evolved a conception of God in some sense to represent the good, which I think can be reduced to what we find as positively reinforcing."[55] In other words, man's conception of God is a personification of what man thinks is good. In behavioral terminology, the good is that which is positively reinforcing. In essence, Skinner is saying that God is made in the image of what man calls good; and what man calls good is whatever induces him to behave in certain ways.[56] Consequently God is identified with positive reinforcers and thus naturalized. So what at first looks like agnosticism on Skinner's part proves on closer examination to be at best a practical atheism.

51. Ibid., p. 19.
52. Skinner, "The Problem of Consciousness—A Debate," *Philosophy and Phenomenological Research* 27, no. 3 (March 1967): 331.
53. Ibid.
54. Cited in a transcript of William F. Buckley's program "Firing Line" (October 17, 1971), p. 8.
55. Ibid., p. 5.
56. Ibid., p. 3.

Further, as was noted earlier, Skinner commends Darwin for his discovery of the role of natural selection, for as a result of this discovery science is able to explain the origin of life on earth "without appealing to a creative mind."[57] Therefore, though Skinner does not rule out the possible existence of God, he does rule out any role God may have played in the creation of life on earth.

Skinner has no use for religion. In fact, in his fictional utopian community, Walden Two, no "religious training" is given to the children, "though parents are free to do so if they wish."[58] Three reasons are given for this attitude toward religion in Walden Two.

First, religion is considered subordinate and even useless to science; hence it is to be ignored as a possible source of knowledge. As Frazier, the behavioral scientist in control of Walden Two, puts it, "Our conception of man is not taken from theology but from a scientific examination of man himself. And we recognize no revealed truths about good or evil or the laws or codes of a successful society."[59] The test for all truth is the experimental test of scientific inquiry—a strict empirical test which is accepted over "all claims of revealed truth."[60]

Second, when the fears and hopes of man which give rise to religion have been, respectively, allayed and fulfilled, religion is rendered useless and vanishes. To quote Frazier again,

> The simple fact is, the religious practices which our members brought to Walden Two have fallen away little by little, like drinking and smoking. . . . Religious faith becomes irrelevant when the fears which nourish it are allayed and the hopes fulfilled—here on earth. . . . [Therefore] we have no need for formal religion, either as ritual or philosophy. But I think we're a devout people in the best sense of that word, and we're far better behaved than any thousand church members taken at random.[61]

Third, the attempt of religion to explain a person's unhappiness by appealing to the concept of need is viewed as desperate and unnecessary. Skinner believes that

57. Skinner, *About Behaviorism*, p. 224.
58. Skinner, *Walden Two*, p. 185.
59. Ibid.
60. Ibid., p. 106.
61. Ibid., p. 185.

we seek solutions to all our problems in the satisfaction of needs. . . .
If those who seem to have everything are still not happy, we are forced
to conclude that there must be less obvious needs which are unsatis-
fied. [For] men must have spiritual as well as material needs—they
must need someone or something beyond themselves to believe in,
and so on—and it is because these needs are unfulfilled that life seems
so often empty and man so often rootless. [But] this desperate move
to preserve the concept of need is unnecessary because a much more
interesting and fruitful design is possible.[62]

This "more interesting and fruitful design" is found in a behavioral
solution to man's unhappiness: "men are happy in an environment
in which active, productive, and creative behavior is reinforced in
effective ways."[63] In short, the answer for man's unhappiness is
found in behaviorism and not in religion.

On top of his rejection of any pragmatic value religion may have,
Skinner proposes that the origin of religious beliefs is the same as
the origin of man's belief in God—that is, they are products of man's
environmental history. Skinner states, for example, that "the Christian
notion of life after death may have grown out of the social reinforcement of those who suffer for their religion while still alive."[64] He offers
a similar explanation for the origin of religious commandments or
laws.[65] Hence as he naturalizes God so he naturalizes religion.

Man's Destiny

Like many, Skinner is greatly concerned about the problems the
world faces today. Such issues as overpopulation, mass starvation,
and the threat of a nuclear holocaust are crying out for resolution,
yet the world seems incapable of offering or effecting adequate solutions. If the present course does not change soon, believes Skinner,
the human race may soon sign its own death certificate. Desiring to
help effect such change, Skinner proposes the abolition of traditional
views of man and the adoption of his behavioral view of man. As he
puts it in About Behaviorism: "Traditional views have been around

62. Skinner, "Contingencies of Reinforcement in the Design of a Culture," in Contemporary Readings in Psychology, p. 450.
63. Ibid.
64. Skinner, Beyond Freedom and Dignity, p. 129.
65. Skinner, About Behaviorism, p. 122.

for centuries, and I think it is fair to say that they have proved to be inadequate. They are largely responsible for the situation in which we now find ourselves." By contrast "behaviorism offers a promising alternative, and I have written this book in an- effort to make its position clear."[66] As Skinner suggests in one of his book titles, we need to go "beyond freedom and dignity," and adopt his behaviorism.

Now to change our view of man to a behavioral perspective is to move forward, but not to move forward far enough. We need to make "vast changes in human behavior" via "a technology of behavior."[67] In doing so we shall abolish such traditional values as freedom and dignity, and in the process adopt the greatest value, namely survival.[68]

Skinner believes that if his behaviorism is adopted, and a behavioral technology is rigorously and universally applied, man could not only save himself but also achieve a utopian world. Skinner claims, "Physical and biological technologies have alleviated pestilence and famine and many painful, dangerous, and exhausting features of daily life, and behavioral technology can begin to alleviate other kinds of ills." Skinner thinks "there are wonderful possibilities—and all the more wonderful because traditional approaches have been so ineffective." He admits, however, that "it is hard to imagine a world in which people live together without quarreling, maintain themselves by producing the food, shelter, and clothing they need, enjoy themselves and contribute to the enjoyment of others," but he confidently adds, "yet all this is possible."[69]

Implicit in all these proposals for effective change is the assumption that man not only must but can control his own destiny. For "man himself may be controlled by his environment, but it is an environment which is almost wholly of his own making."[70] Hence "man as we know him, for better or for worse, is what man has made of man."[71]

Skinner holds that his behavioral humanism, if implemented in time, can save man from self-annihilation, but adds that it will only preserve him for annihilation by a different adversary. "The human species," he says, "will never reach a final state of perfection before

66. Ibid., p. 8.
67. Skinner, *Beyond Freedom and Dignity*, pp. 2 – 3.
68. Ibid., pp. 130, 173.
69. Ibid., pp. 204 – 205.
70. Ibid., p. 196.
71. Ibid., p. 197.

it is exterminated—'some say in fire, some in ice,' and some in radiation."[72] The same nonrational, purposeless forces which brought man into existence and shaped all his behavior will one day snuff him out of existence. A Skinnerian salvation, no matter how effective, could only delay the annihilation of the human race—it could not stop it.

An Evaluation of Behavioral Humanism

Ever since its first printed formulations Skinner's behavioral humanism has won a significant number of converts and has sparked a great deal of controversy. There is much to be said regarding his position, some of which is positive and much of which is negative. Some brief comments on both sides will be made here.

Some Positive Features

Skinner is to be commended for pointing out the often powerful influence a person's culture has on his behavior. From childhood to adulthood, parents, peer groups, the mass media, teachers, and various governmental and religious organizations all contribute to the shaping of one's behavior. It is a fact of life that a child grows up emulating those around him he most admires, and as a consequence often behaves like them throughout his adult life.

Secondly, Skinner should also be given credit for his genuine concern for mankind as a whole. It is very easy, especially in an affluent nation like the United States, to be concerned only for one's own needs and desires, and not for those of others. However, Skinner is not only concerned for the other person, but has worked diligently to find ways to improve the human situation.

Finally, Skinner's unwillingness to accept any truth claim unless it can be justified is also commendable. A rational, sane, sober man does not willingly step into an airplane if he has good reason to believe that the pilot is too drunk to safely fly the plane. Neither should such a person believe in any truth claim unless he has good reasons to believe that the claim is really true. For what someone might claim is true is not necessarily true. For example, one can

72. Ibid., p. 199.

claim there is biological life on other planets, but the careful scientist will want some evidence for this before he accepts it as true. Hence one should have sufficient grounds for believing a claim to be true before he actually places his trust in that claim.

Some Criticisms

Skinner's behavioral humanism is open to a number of criticisms, some of which are briefly noted here.

First, his position is reductionistic. For example, he reduces human thought to human behavior and morality to the environment. However, such "nothing but" statements require "more than" knowledge. That is, in order for Skinner to know that human thought is "nothing but" human behavior, his own knowledge of human thought must go beyond, (i.e., must be "more than") his own behavior. This, of course, would defeat his claim that all human thought (which includes his own) is nothing but or nothing more than human behavior. Skinner denies the charge that his behaviorism is reductionistic, claiming that "it simply provides an alternative account of the same facts." For example, in the case of human thought, his view "does not *reduce* thought processes to behavior; it simply analyzes the behavior previously explained by the invention of thought processes."[73] But how can Skinner know that thought processes are invented explanations for behavior unless he knows more than merely behavior? And if he knows more than behavior then his behaviorism is wrong.

Second, Skinner's belief that all human thought is a product of nonrational causes makes all human thought nonrational. All thinking is therefore illogical and invalid. According to such a view no truth claim could be known to be true or false. In fact Skinner insists that it is a fallacy to believe "in truth or falsity or any of the other truth value systems which logic has proposed."[74] If this is indeed the case, then one could never know if Skinner's behavioral humanism is true or false. Indeed, to attempt to determine whether it is true or not would be to assume a rational basis for thought—but for Skinner all human thought is nonrational. In brief, Skinner's behaviorism is true or false or neither. If it is true, then it is self-defeating, for it claims to demonstrate as true that there is no such thing as truth.

73. Skinner, *About Behaviorism*, pp. 240 – 241.
74. Cited in Buckley's "Firing Line," p. 10.

If it is false, then we can reject it as such and move on to other proposals. And if it is neither true nor false, then it is no view at all, since it is making no truth claim.

Third, Skinner's claim that man is completely determined is self-defeating. For according to Skinner both determinists (like himself) and nondeterminists are behaviorally determined to believe what they believe. Yet Skinner writes to convince nondeterminists that they are wrong and that, as reasonable men, they ought to accept determinism. However, this implies that they are free to reject non-determinism and accept determinism. But this kind of freedom is what Skinner denies. Hence, Skinner's approach implies what it denies. It is self-defeating.

Fourth, although Skinner finds religion per se useless once man's needs and fears are taken care of, he still makes use of religious practices. This pragmatic use of religion is spelled out more fully in *Walden Two*. Says Frazier,

> We've borrowed some of the practices of organized religion—to inspire group loyalty and strengthen the observance of the code. I believe I've mentioned our Sunday meetings. There's usually some sort of music, sometimes religious. And a philosophical, poetic, or religious work is read or acted out. We like the effect of this upon the speech of the community. It gives us a common stock of literary allusions. Then there's a brief "lesson"—of the utmost importance in maintaining an observance of the code. Usually items are chosen for discussion which deal with self-control and certain kinds of social articulation.[75]

Thus even the materialistic humanist reveals a need for religion.

Fifth, Skinner has a serious inconsistency in his position. On the one hand he claims man is completely determined and not free. Yet on the other hand he exhorts man to change his environment, for he says things like, "Man ... is what man has made of man,"[76] and man's environment "is an environment which is almost wholly of his own making."[77] But Skinner cannot have it both ways. If man is completely determined by his environment, then man cannot be determining his environment.

Furthermore, why does Skinner urge man to act to save himself

---

75. Skinner, *Walden Two*, p. 185.
76. Skinner, *Beyond Freedom and Dignity*, p. 197.
77. Ibid., p. 196.

from destruction if there is not an implied "you can do it" in all of this? Skinner's very exhortations imply a belief that man ought to (and can) act to change his environment. But if man were completely determined as Skinner claims, he could not do this. Thus what Skinner claims and what he implies are incompatible.

Sixth, Skinner's view has serious ethical problems. In *Walden Two*, Frazier, one of the main controllers, admits to being a behavioral dictator who is not indifferent to power and who likes to play God.[78]

This raises a further question: who is to control the controllers? After all, could not a despotic behavioral tyrant get control of the reins and make the controlled do as he wanted? Skinner assents that such could happen but believes it is very unlikely. In any case, to guard against such an occurrence effective countercontrols must be arranged so as to "bring some important consequences to bear on the behavior of the controller."[79] Restating this proposed solution, Howard W. Ferrin puts it well: "So the controller controls the controlled, but, to make sure he does not over-control the controlled, the controlled control the controller! Feel better now?"[80]

This raises still a further question: who is to arrange the needed countercontrols? To this Skinner answers that it is not who but what will arrange them:

> It will not be a benevolent dictator, a compassionate therapist, a devoted teacher, or a public-spirited industrialist who will design a way of life in the interests of everyone. We must look instead at the conditions under which people govern, give help, teach, and arrange incentive systems in particular ways. In other words we must look to the culture as a social environment.[81]

We thus come full circle on the question of control. Even though Skinner says behavioral technicians should be the controllers and they in turn should be members of the group they control, ultimately no individual or group of individuals controls or countercontrols anything unless the all-controlling environment causes them to do so. In the final analysis only whats, not whos, are in control.

78. Skinner, *Walden Two*, pp. 278 – 282.

79. Skinner, *Beyond Freedom and Dignity*, p. 163.

80. Howard W. Ferrin, "Manipulation or Motivation? Skinner's Utopia vs. Jesus' Kingdom," in *Christianity Today*, 29 September 1972, p. 9.

81. Skinner, *About Behaviorism*, p. 206.

3

Existential Humanism

Humanism comes in several varieties. Some humanists stress the value of the human race (e.g., Erich Fromm). Others place heavy emphasis on the value of the individual (e.g., Jean-Paul Sartre). It is the latter group that is the subject of this chapter. While behavioral humanists such as B. F. Skinner have stressed the deterministic factors of man's environment, the existential humanists have emphasized man's irrevocable freedom.

What Is Existentialism?

Before we can understand what an existential form of humanism is we must first define existentialism. The term *existentialism* comes from the word *existence*. Hence an existentialist stresses the conditions of human existence. He believes that the concrete is more important than the abstract, that doing is more important than being (or essence). Thus the fundamental thesis of the existentialist is that "existence is prior to essence." But while truth is found in the concrete, it is at the same time always personal and not merely propositional. Unless one believes something subjectively and passionately, he does not possess the truth. From this perspective subjectivity is prior to (or more important than) objectivity, choosing is prior to thinking. In fact, in Sartre's form of existentialism heavy stress is placed on individual human freedom.

What Is Existential Humanism?

Not all existentialists are humanists. In fact the father of modern existentialism, Sören Kierkegaard (d. 1855), was a Christian. Conversely, not all humanists are existentialists. As the topics of other chapters indicate, there are scientific, economic, materialistic, and even religious forms of humanism. What then is unique about an existential kind of humanism?

According to Sartre there are two kinds of humanism: one he opposes and the other he favors. First, "one may understand by humanism a theory which upholds man as the end-in-itself and the supreme value." Sartre rejects this kind of humanism. He opts for a humanism in which "man is all the time outside of himself." For "it is by pursuing transcendent aims that he himself is able to exist." That is, since there is no universe other than the universe of human subjectivity, "we remind man that there is no legislator but himself; that he himself, thus abandoned, must decide for himself." So "by seeking, beyond himself . . . man can realize himself as truly human."[1] This is what Sartre means by "existential humanism."

The Characteristics of Sartre's Existential Humanism

For the sake of simplicity we will discuss Sartre's view in several categories. We will begin with his humanistic view of God and then speak of man, ethics, and human destiny.

Sartre's Humanistic View of "God"

Sartre is an atheist. He believes there is no God, and offers several reasons for this conclusion. First of all, God by definition is a self-caused being. He cannot be caused by another or else He would not be God. But, insists Sartre, a self-caused being is impossible by its very nature. Hence, there cannot be a God.[2] Why is it impossible to be self-caused? Because a cause is prior to its effect (in being, not in time), and one cannot be prior to himself.

Further Sartre believes that man is free—absolutely free. The proof of this is that man can say no to anything. Thus, Sartre suggests, the French were never so free as when the Germans occupied France

1. Jean-Paul Sartre, *Existentialism and Humanism*, trans. Philip Mairet (London: Methuen, 1948), pp. 55 – 56.
2. Sartre, *Being and Nothingness*, trans. Hazel E. Barnes (New York: Washington Square, 1965), pp. 758 – 759.

during World War II. For even though they were forced on the outside (objectively) to accept German rule, nevertheless they were free on the inside (subjectively) to reject it. Likewise, a person is free to reject his past. For one always transcends what he has been. "I am" is always over "I was." In this same sense, believes Sartre, "*I* am not *me.*" For "I" (as subject) transcend myself or "me" (as object). Put yourself ("me") in a test tube and look in at your "self" as an object. What you discover in the process—out of the corner of your eye, as it were—is that as you view your self ("me") there is always an "I" doing the viewing which cannot itself be viewed. For if you begin to think about the "I" it becomes a "me" (object) of the "I" which is always viewing but can never be viewed. Hence, my subjectivity always transcends my objectivity; I am absolutely free.

But if I am free—absolutely free—then God cannot exist. For if God exists then He determines all things. But I undeniably and absolutely determine myself. Therefore, if I am, then God is not. I am. Hence God is not. In Sartre's own words, "there is no God and no prevenient design, which can adapt the world and all its possibilities to my will."[3]

Sartre's Humanistic View of Man

Sartre recognizes that if God is dead then whatever man is, he is alone. Sartre writes, "There was nothing left in heaven . . . nor anyone to give me orders. . . . I am doomed to have no other law but mine."[4]

But what precisely is man according to Sartre? In his words, "man is the being whose project is to become God." For "to be man means to reach toward being God."[5] In what way? Well, God is by definition a self-caused being, and man's fundamental goal in life is to be self-determined. In Sartre's words, man is the "being-for-itself" that desires to become the "being-in-itself." That is, man is freedom wanting to become determined or the subject wanting to objectify himself.

It is of course impossible for man to objectify himself. Hence man is in essence absurd. He is nothing desiring to be something, the contingent seeking to be necessary. In reality man is an empty bubble

---

3. Sartre, *Existentialism and Humanism*, p. 39.
4. Sartre, *The Flies*, in *No Exit and Three Other Plays*, trans. Stuart Gilbert (New York: Vintage, 1947), pp. 121 – 123.
5. Sartre, *Being and Nothingness*, p. 694.

floating on a sea of nothingness. In fact, man really has no essence. "Man is nothing else but that which he makes of himself." Thus "there is no human nature, because there is no God to have a conception of it. Man simply is."[6]

Not only is man locked into futility, but he is also condemned to freedom. He is absurdly free. In fact, he cannot not be free. "I am my freedom," Sartre wrote. "No sooner had you [Zeus] created me than I ceased to be yours. I was like a man who's lost his shadow. And there was nothing left in heaven, no right or wrong, nor anyone to give me orders." However, "I shall not return under your law; I am doomed to have no other law but mine.... For I, Zeus, am a man, and every man must find his own way."[7] So then, "choice is possible, but what is not possible is not to choose."[8]

Sartre's Humanistic View of Ethics

The best choice one can make is to become a heroic atheist. And since there are no objective or eternal values, each person must create his own values. In the last lines of his famous book *Being and Nothingness* Sartre wrote, "All human activities are equivalent.... Thus it amounts to the same thing whether one gets drunk alone or is a leader of nations."[9] Consequently ethics must begin in despair; it must, in Sartre's words, "repudiate the spirit of seriousness" which believes in transcendent values.[10]

Despite this apparently pessimistic tone Sartre insists that his ethics is really optimistic. For it begins in despair, but it need not end there. Absurdity is only the starting point and not the final conclusion. Thus it is essentially an ethics of ambiguity.[11]

To be sure, there are no objective or eternal values. Man does not discover values; he creates them. And even though his attempt to be God is vain, nevertheless in the process man becomes man and this is not vain. So even though man cannot be right with God, he can

6. Sartre, *Existentialism and Humanism*, p. 28.
7. Sartre, *The Flies*, pp. 121 – 123.
8. Sartre, *Existentialism and Humanism*, p. 48.
9. Sartre, *Being and Nothingness*, p. 627.
10. Ibid., p. 626.
11. See Simone de Beauvoir, *The Ethics of Ambiguity*, trans. Bernard Frechtman (New York: Philosophical Library, 1948), pp. 10, 16 – 18, 156.

in a sense be right with himself. Thus God's absence does not authorize license; it establishes responsibility.[12]

Sartre believes, contrary to his opponents, that "what is annoying them is not so much our pessimism, but more likely, our optimism." For "what is alarming in the doctrine [is] that it confronts man with a possibility of choice."[13] That is to say, "the first effect of existentialism is that it puts every man in possession of himself as he is, and places the entire responsibility for his existence squarely upon his own shoulders." And "when we say that man is responsible for himself, we do not mean that he is responsible only for his own individuality, but that he is responsible for all men."[14] For instance, if "I decide to marry and to have children, . . . I am thereby committing not only myself, but humanity as a whole, to the practice of monogamy."[15] Hence when one acts with his individual freedom he is "at the same time a legislator deciding for the whole of mankind—in such a moment a man cannot escape from the sense of complete and profound responsibility." Thus "every man ought to say, 'am I really a man who has the right to act in such a manner that humanity regulates itself by what I do?' "[16]

By the "obligation" to act for all men Sartre does not mean an obligation imposed by another or a divine duty. "The existentialist, on the contrary, finds it extremely embarrassing that God does not exist." For "there disappears with Him all possibility of finding value in an intelligible heaven. . . . It is nowhere written that 'the good' exists, that one must be honest or must not be, since we are now upon the plane where there are only men." As Dostoevski once wrote, "If God did not exist, everything would be permitted; and that, for existentialism, is the starting point."[17] And further, Sartre notes that "if God does not exist, [we are not] provided with any values or commands that could legitimate our behavior. . . . We are left alone, without excuse. That is what I mean when I say that man is condemned to be free." Man is "condemned, because he did not create himself, yet is nevertheless at liberty, and from the moment that he

12. Ibid., pp. 11 – 16.
13. Sartre, Existentialism and Humanism, p. 25.
14. Ibid., p. 29.
15. Ibid., p. 30.
16. Ibid., p. 32.
17. Quoted in Sartre, Existentialism, p. 33.

is thrown into this world he is responsible for everything he does."[18] In short, man is responsible—wholly responsible—for what he does, but he is not responsible to God or any externally imposed moral law. He is responsible solely to himself. And even though when man acts he is obliged to act for mankind, nonetheless this is only a self-imposed obligation. There is no divine duty to do good to others.

Sartre's Humanistic View of Man's Destiny

Existential humanism does not have a developed eschatology. And contrary to liberal or utopian forms of humanism it does not expect a better future. Sartre frankly admits, "We do not believe in progress. Progress implies amelioration; but man is always the same."[19] Man's ultimate end is not millennial (forward-looking) or spiritual (upward-looking); it is volitional. "The actions of men of good faith have, as their ultimate significance, the quest of freedom itself as such." For, says Sartre, "I declare that freedom ... can have no other end and aim but itself." The absurd and futile world will continue. Man will continue to find himself thrust into it—condemned to the inescapability of his own absolute freedom. For this he must assume full responsibility, even though achieving a better future through the exercise of that freedom is an impossibility.

An Evaluation of Existential Humanism

Humanists are so diverse in their points of view that the affirmation of one form of humanism is the negation of another form.

Sartre's Criticism of Humanism

Sartre, for example, proffers a severe critique of the kind of humanism which makes man an end or ultimate. He writes, "That kind of humanism is absurd, for only the dog or the horse would be in a position to pronounce a general judgment upon man and declare that he is magnificent, which they have never been such fools as to do—at least not as far as I know." It is inadmissible for man to

18. Ibid., p. 34.
19. Ibid., p. 50.

pronounce such a judgment on himself. Furthermore, "an existentialist will never take man as an end, since man is still to be determined." To set up man as an end is cultic. And "the cult of humanity ends in Comtian humanism, shut-in upon itself, and—this must be said—in Fascism. We do not want a humanism like that."[20]

But, we may ask, although Sartre's own kind of humanism avoids Fascism, does it evade nihilism? Certainly it is the negation of all objective and eternal values, and also of all divine duty. With this Sartre himself feels uneasy. He speaks of atheism as "a cruel and long-range affair."[21] In point of fact, does Sartre avoid radical subjectivism? If the only values and obligations I have are those I will to have, then they can also be destroyed by my will. If values are created by me they can also be eliminated by me.

Further, according to Sartre, what I will for myself I ought to will for others. But two problems emerge here. First, this "ought" is not really ethically binding; it is, as Sartre admits, only a logical (not an axiological) "ought." Second, what if one wills suicide for himself? According to Sartre he should thereby will it for all men. Actually Sartre says that one should not commit suicide. For the act of "freedom" by which one destroys his freedom is not proper for an existentialist who believes freedom is the "essence" of man. Any act against itself cannot be an act for itself.[22] But if this is the case, then freedom, the freedom of every man, is an absolute. And men are an end in themselves after all. Thus Sartre (a man) has pronounced men—all men—to be an absolute end. In this sense Sartre does not escape his own criticism: it is inadmissible for man to pronounce such a judgment on himself.

A Criticism of Sartre's Humanism

It should be noted here that Sartre's attempt to eliminate God is seriously flawed. First of all, he constructs a straw God by defining Him as "self-caused." Most theists do not believe God is a self-caused being; they hold God to be an uncaused being.[23] A self-caused being

20. Ibid., pp. 54 – 55.

21. Sartre, *Words* (New York: George Braziller, 1964), p. 253.

22. Sartre, *Being and Nothingness*, pp. 479, 556, 762, 766.

23. See Norman L. Geisler, *Philosophy of Religion* (Grand Rapids: Zondervan, 1974), chap. 9; and *Christian Apologetics* (Grand Rapids: Baker, 1976), chaps. 12 – 13, for a further discussion.

is impossible, as Sartre points out. But an uncaused being is not impossible, at least not on Sartrian grounds. For Sartre speaks of man as "thrust" or "given"; man is simply "there" without cause, reason, or justification. But if man can be uncaused then certainly God could be as well.

Second, how can man be "given" without a Giver or "thrust" without a Thruster? As even the skeptic David Hume admitted, it is absurd to believe that things arise without a cause.[24] Surely the existential "pot" is calling the theistic "kettle" black when Sartre speaks of the Christian God as an incoherent concept! What is more incoherent than to believe that man comes to be without a cause?

Third, does freedom really eliminate God? Certainly absolute human freedom would be incompatible with the traditional notion of God. For absolute freedom would be God, since only God can have absolute freedom. So if man is absolutely free—free to create any and all values—then God must go. Sartre once said, "Since we ignore the commandments of God [concerning] all value prescribed as eternal, nothing remains but what is strictly voluntary."[25] But in reality it was, as we shall see, the other way around. That is, Sartre affirmed his own freedom in the face of the God who was there, and as a consequence God left him.

Fourth, Sartre's atheism began in rebellion against God. As is the case with most atheists, Sartre once believed in God. In his autobiography he tells how he became an atheist:

> I had been playing with matches and burned a small rug. I was in the process of covering up my crime when suddenly God saw me. I felt His gaze inside my head and on my hands. . . . I flew into a rage against so crude an indiscretion, I blasphemed. . . . He never looked at me again. . . . I had the more difficulty getting rid of Him [the Holy Ghost] in that He had installed Himself at the back of my head. . . . I collared the Holy Ghost in the cellar and threw Him out.[26]

Sartre's basic irrationalism reveals itself when he admits that he would reject "even a valid proof of the existence of God." This is reminiscent of Friedrich Nietzsche's confession that "we deny God

---

24. See David Hume, *The Letters of David Hume*, ed. J. Y. T. Grieg (Oxford: Clarendon, 1932), 1:187.
25. Sartre, *Existentialism and Humanism*, pp. 23 – 24.
26. Sartre, *Words*, pp. 102, 252 – 253.

as God. If one were to *prove* this God of the Christians to us, we should be even less able to believe in him."[27]

Fifth, Sartre has a basic inconsistency in his existentialism. He denies absolute value and truth and yet he affirms both. He speaks of human subjectivity and freedom as "the absolute truth of consciousness as it attains to itself."[28] He adds, "There must be an absolute truth, and there is such a truth which is simple, easily attained and within the reach of everybody; it consists in one's immediate sense of one's self."

Likewise, in the realm of value Sartre speaks of an "absolute commitment" and of "universal value."[29] At one point Sartre clearly oversteps his own self-imposed value of not making value judgments on another, admitting that "here one cannot avoid pronouncing a judgment of truth." Sartre unconvincingly hedges his judgment: "It is not for me to judge him morally, but I define his self-deception as an error."[30] But is not the judgment that one is wrong to engage in self-deception a moral judgment? There are two reasons that it does not help for Sartre to claim that he has made only a truth-judgment. First, it is obviously Sartre's view that one ought not reject the truth. But "ought" here is a moral judgment. Second, making an absolute truth-judgment about others is contrary to a system that rejects all absolutes beyond its own freedom. To be consistent Sartre should make no value or truth-judgments about others. But he does. And therein lies a basic inconsistency in his form of humanism.

Finally, Sartre himself had second thoughts about his system. In the spring of 1980 (only weeks before his death) Sartre is reported to have said, "I do not feel that I am the product of chance, a speck of dust in the universe, but someone who was expected, prepared, prefigured. In short, a being whom only a Creator could put here; and this idea of a creating hand refers to God." Sartre's mistress, Simone de Beauvoir, reacted critically to Sartre's apparent recantation, complaining, "How should one explain this senile act of a turncoat?" She added, "All my friends, all the Sartrians, and the editorial

27. Friedrich Nietzsche, *Antichrist*, in *The Portable Nietzsche*, ed. and trans. Walter Kaufmann (New York: Viking, 1968), p. 627.
28. Sartre, *Existentialism and Humanism*, p. 44.
29. Ibid., pp. 46 – 47.
30. Ibid., p. 51.

team of *Les Temps Modernes* supported me in my consternation."[31] If true, well should his existential colleagues have reacted this way, for the apparent recantation is a condemnation of Sartrian humanism by Sartre himself.[32]

31. From a dialogue with a Marxist recorded in the *Nouvel Observateur,* as reported by Thomas Molnor, *National Review,* 11 June 1982, p. 677.

32. Alain Larrey and Michael Viguier, two young men living in Paris, confirmed in a letter to the author that two months before his death Sartre had admitted to his Catholic doctor that he "regretted the impact his writings had on youth" and that so many had "taken them so seriously."

4

Pragmatic Humanism

John Dewey has been called the father of American education. His philosophy has affected virtually every American on a practical level. In this regard his humanistic influence can scarcely be overestimated; thus no discussion of humanism would be complete without including his pragmatic form of humanism.

The Origin and Nature of Man

Like many humanists Dewey rejected belief in the traditional God. One of the reasons he did so was the rise of the modern scientific understanding of the world. For Dewey the impact of modern science made belief in a supernatural origin of the universe untenable: "The impact of astronomy eliminated the older religious creation stories." And "geological discoveries have displaced creation myths which once bulked large." In addition, "biology has revolutionized conceptions of soul and mind . . . and this science has made a profound impression upon ideas of sin, redemption, and immortality." Furthermore, "anthropology, history and literary criticism have furnished a radically different version of the historic events and personages upon which Christian religions have built." Finally, Dewey believed that "psychology is already opening to us natural explanations of phenomena so extraordinary that once their supernatural origin was, so to say, the natural explanation."[1]

As a result of the innovations of modern science Dewey believed

1. John Dewey, *A Common Faith* (New Haven, Conn.: Yale University, 1934), p. 31.

even agnosticism was too mild a reaction to traditional theism. For "'agnosticism' is a shadow cast by the eclipse of the supernatural,"[2] and "generalized agnosticism is only a halfway elimination of the supernatural." In traditional terms Dewey was an atheist. He rejected any attempt to support the existence of God, saying, "The cause of the dissatisfaction is perhaps not so much the arguments that Kant used to show the insufficiency of these alleged proofs, as it is the growing feeling that they are too formal to offer any support to religion in action."[3] Like most antitheists, Dewey believed the reality of evil cannot be reconciled with the concept of a personal, good, and all-powerful being (God).[4]

Another factor in Dewey's rejection of belief in God was the rise of modern secularism, which began with the Renaissance and continued in the eighteenth century's protest against ecclesiastical authority. Dewey saw secularism as coming to fruition in the nineteenth-century "diffusion of the supernatural through secular life."[5] Secular interests grew up independently of organized religion. And now, said Dewey, "the hold of these interests upon the thought and desires of men has crowded the social importance of organized religions into a corner and the area of this corner is decreasing."[6]

Since modern man thinks in scientific and secular terms, Dewey took a naturalistic view of the origin of man. Man is a result of naturalistic evolutionary processes, not a special creation by any kind of God.

The Nature of the Religious

Dewey was dead set against any form of supernaturalism in religion. In fact, since most religions pay some homage to the supernatural, he was also opposed to religion in general.

The Elimination of the Supernatural and Religion

Dewey made no bones about the fact that belief in any form of supernaturalism had to go:

2. Ibid., p. 86.
3. Ibid., p. 11.
4. Ibid., p. 45.
5. Ibid., p. 65.
6. Ibid., p. 83.

If I have said anything about religions and religion that seems harsh, I have said those things because of a firm belief that the claim on the part of religions to possess a monopoly of ideas and of the supernatural means by which alone, it is alleged, they can be furthered, stands in the way of the realization of distinctively religious values inherent in natural experience.[7]

He gives several reasons for rejecting the supernatural:

1. Not only is belief in the supernatural based on ignorance, but it also hinders social intelligence. For "it stifles the growth of the social intelligence by means of which the direction of social change could be taken out of the region of accident."[8]

2. Science calls into question the very concept of the supernatural.[9] Many things once thought to be miraculous are now known to have natural explanations. Science will continue to explain the unusual phenomena of nature.

3. Belief in the supernatural hinders social progress. For "men have never fully used the powers they possess to advance the good in life, because they have waited upon some power external to themselves and to nature to do the work they are responsible for doing. Dependence upon an external power is the counterpart of surrender of human endeavor."[10]

4. Not only is social progress hindered by belief in the supernatural, but social values are actually depreciated by it. "The contention of an increasing number of persons is that depreciation of natural social values has resulted, both in principle and in actual fact, from reference of their origin and significance to supernatural sources."[11]

5. Finally, even truly religious attitudes are hampered by belief in the supernatural. Dewey wrote, "I have suggested that the religious element in life has been hampered by conceptions of the supernatural that were imbedded in those cultures wherein man had little control over outer nature and little in the way of sure method of inquiry and test."[12]

7. Ibid., pp. 27 – 28.
8. Ibid., p. 78.
9. Ibid., p. 38.
10. Ibid., p. 46.
11. Ibid., p. 71.
12. Ibid., p. 56.

Despite Dewey's rejection of the supernatural he was by no means irreligious. In fact he insisted on the need for and preservation of the religious. What Dewey proposed was that religion as traditionally defined—as involving belief in the supernatural beyond this life—be discarded for a religious attitude toward all of life:

> I shall develop another conception of the nature of the religious phase of experience, one that separates it from the supernatural and the things that have grown up about it. I shall try to show that these derivations are encumbrances and that what is genuinely religious will undergo an emancipation when it is relieved from them; that then, for the first time, the religious aspect of experience will be free to develop freely on its own account.[13]

Dewey offers several reasons for rejecting religion:

1. One problem with traditional religion, as Dewey saw it, was its sacred-secular split. But

> The conception that "religious" signifies a certain attitude and outlook, independent of the supernatural, necessitates no such division. It does not shut religious values up within a particular compartment, nor assume that a particular form of association bears a unique relation to it. Upon the social side the future of the religious function seems preeminently bound up with its emancipation from religions and a particular religion.[14]

2. All religions "involve specific intellectual beliefs, and they attach . . . importance to assent[ing] to these doctrines as true, true in an intellectual sense." That is, "they have developed a doctrinal apparatus it is incumbent upon 'believers' . . . to accept."[15]

3. Further, "there is nothing left worth preserving in the notions of the unseen powers, [which control] human destiny [and] to which obedience, reverence and worship are due." For such a definition applies equally to both noble ideals and "the most savage and degraded beliefs and practices."[16]

4. Actually "we are forced to acknowledge that concretely there is no such thing as religion in the singular. There is only a multitude

13. Ibid., p. 2.
14. Ibid., pp. 66 – 67.
15. Ibid., p. 29.
16. Ibid., p. 7.

of religions."[17] For the various modes and motives of worship have no discernible common denominator for the concept of "God."

5. The most basic reason, however, is that religion hinders social progress. It involves belief in the supernatural, which, as has already been seen, is a hindrance to achievement of socially desirable goals.

According to Dewey nothing is lost with the elimination of religion. In fact, since more people are religious than have a religion, there is much to be gained by rejecting religion. For, said Dewey, "I believe that many persons are so repelled from what exists as a religion by its intellectual and moral implications, that they are not even aware of attitudes in themselves that if they came to fruition would be genuinely religious."[18]

The Establishment of Natural Religious Attitudes

John Dewey was quick to point out that he was not proposing that we replace supernatural religion with a natural religion:

> I am not proposing a religion, but rather the emancipation of elements and outlooks that may be called religious. For the moment we have a religion, ... the ideal factors in experience that may be called religious take on a load that is not inherent in them, a load of current beliefs and of institutional practices that are irrelevant to them.[19]

The difference between a religion and the religious is that a religion "always signifies a special body of beliefs and practices having some kind of institutional organization, loose or tight." By contrast "the adjective 'religious' denotes nothing in the way of a specifiable entity, either institutional or as a system of beliefs." Rather, "it denotes an attitude that may be taken toward every object and every proposed end or ideal."[20]

The definition of the religious

The result of rejecting traditional religious beliefs for religious attitudes is a new adjustment and orientation to life. Thus Dewey's humanistic definition of the religious is as follows: "Any activity pur-

17. Ibid.
18. Ibid., p. 9.
19. Ibid., p. 8.
20. Ibid., pp. 9 – 10.

sued in behalf of an ideal end against obstacles and in spite of threats of personal loss because of conviction of its general and enduring value is religious in quality."[21]

Dewey acknowledges with Friedrich Schleiermacher that a religious experience involves a feeling of dependence. But he insists it must be a dependence without traditional doctrines or fear. For "fear never gave stable perspective in the life of anyone."[22] Actually religious experience helps to develop a sense of unity that would be impossible without it. For by means of a religious experience "the self is always directed toward something beyond itself and so its own unification depends upon the idea of the integration of the shifting scenes of the world into that imaginative totality we call the Universe."[23]

Religious experience takes place in different ways in different people. "It is sometimes brought about by devotion to a cause; sometimes by a passage of poetry that opens a new perspective; sometimes as was the case with Spinoza ... through philosophical reflection." So religious experiences do not necessarily occur in isolation. Rather, "they occur frequently in connection with many significant moments of living."[24] Religious experience is a kind of unifying ideal of other experiences in life.

The definition of "God"

John Dewey was willing to use the term *God*. But for him it did not mean a supernatural being but "the ideal ends that at a given time and place one acknowledges as having authority over his volition and emotion, the values to which one is supremely devoted, as far as these ends, through imagination, take on unity."[25] That is, the idea of "God" represents a unification of one's essential values. For Dewey progress and achievement were such ideal values.

Dewey believed that it was essential that persons have such religious ideas. For "neither observation, thought, nor practical activity can attain that complete unification of the self which is called a whole. The *whole* self is an ideal, an imaginative projection."[26] Thus

21. Ibid., p. 27.
22. Ibid., p. 25.
23. Ibid., p. 19.
24. Ibid., p. 14.
25. Ibid., p. 42.
26. Ibid., p. 19.

self-unification can be achieved only through a religious commitment to "God" (that is, to ideal values). Said Dewey, "I should describe this faith as the unification of the self through allegiance to inclusive ideal ends, which imagination presents to us and to which the human will responds as worthy of controlling our desires and choices."[27]

A common faith of mankind

Dewey intended his religious form of pragmatic humanism to be practiced worldwide. In his "common faith" he saw a religious goal for all mankind. "Here are all the elements for a religious faith that shall not be confined to sect, class, or race. Such a faith has always been implicitly the common faith of mankind. It remains to make it explicit and militant."[28] In this connection he saw the doctrine of the brotherhood of all men as having great religious significance. He believed that more than lip service must be given to "the idea of the common brotherhood of all men." For "whether or not we are, save in some metaphorical sense, all brothers, we are at least in the same boat traversing the same turbulent ocean. The potential religious significance of this fact is infinite."[29]

Dedication to Human Progress

Religion: A Hindrance to Social Progress

One reason Dewey was strongly opposed to traditional supernatural religion was that he perceived it to be a hindrance to social progress: "the assumption that only supernatural agencies can give control is a sure method of retarding this effort [of social betterment]."[30]

Dewey saw three stages in social development. "In the first stage, human relationships were thought to be so infected with the evils of corrupt human nature as to require redemption from external and supernatural sources." Dewey felt that man had to move past this stage. "In the next stage, what is significant in these relations is found to be akin to values esteemed distinctively religious." Man must move

27. Ibid., p. 33.
28. Ibid., p. 87.
29. Ibid., p. 84.
30. Ibid., p. 76.

past this stage as well. "The third stage would realize that in fact the values prized in those religions that have ideal elements are idealizations of things characteristic of natural association which have been projected into a supernatural realm for safekeeping and sanction." Dewey warned, "Unless there is a movement into what I have called the third stage, fundamental dualism and a division in life continue."[31]

Science: The Means to Human Progress

According to Dewey man must achieve his own social progress. This belief is neither egoistic nor optimistic. "It is not the first, for it does not isolate man, either individually or collectively, from nature." And "it is not the second, because it makes no assumption beyond that of the need and responsibility for human endeavor. . . . It involves no expectation of a millennium of good."[32]

The only adequate means of achieving the goal of social progress is science. Dewey claims, "One of the few experiments in the attachment of emotion to ends that mankind has not tried is that of devotion, so intense as to be religious, to intelligence as a force in social action."[33] He states further, "There is but one sure road of access to truth—the road of patient, cooperative inquiry operating by means of observation, experimental record and controlled reflection."[34] "Were we to admit that there is but one method for ascertaining fact and truth—that conveyed by the word 'scientific' in its most general and generous sense—no discovery in any branch of knowledge and inquiry could then disturb the faith that is religious."[35]

For Dewey faith in science, that is, in the critical intelligence, is more religious than faith in any revelation from God. For "faith in the continued disclosing of truth through directed cooperative human endeavor is more religious in quality than is any faith in a completed revelation." While on the one hand "some fixed doctrinal apparatus is necessary for a religion . . . faith in the possibilities of continued and rigorous inquiry does not limit access to truth to any channel or scheme of things." Dewey notes that this religious nature of faith

31. Ibid., p. 73.
32. Ibid., p. 46.
33. Ibid., p. 79.
34. Ibid., p. 32.
35. Ibid., p. 33.

in science makes some proponents of religion uneasy: "There is such a thing as faith in intelligence becoming religious in quality—a fact that perhaps explains the efforts of some religionists to disparage the possibilities of intelligence as a force. They properly feel such faith to be a dangerous rival."[36]

Science has a decided advantage over religion as a means for human progress. For "science is not constituted by any particular body of subject-matter. It is constituted by a method, a method of changing beliefs by means of tested inquiry as well as arriving at them." As a matter of fact, not only is science superior to religious dogma, it is opposed to it. "For scientific method is adverse not only to dogma but to doctrine as well, provided we take 'doctrine' in its usual meaning—a body of definite beliefs that need only to be taught and learned as true." However, "this negative attitude of science to doctrine does not indicate indifference to truth. It signifies supreme loyalty to the method by which truth is attained. The scientific-religious conflict ultimately is a conflict between allegiance to this method and allegiance to an irreducible minimum of belief so fixed in advance that it can never be modified."[37] Hence science and religion are irreconcilable. But a religious dedication and science are not—in fact a religious dedication to science is essential to human progress.

An Evaluation of Pragmatic Humanism

Dewey's pragmatic humanism has much in common with many other forms of humanism. It is naturalistic, relativistic, and optimistic; and despite its opposition to religion, it is even religious. There are, however, some characteristics peculiar to Dewey. Dewey's form of humanism is pragmatic, melioristic (progressive), and democratic. Also, Dewey places great emphasis on science (critical intelligence) as the means for human achievement. His definition of God as the ideal, unifying goal for human progress is also unique. In short, Dewey believes that man's salvation is by education. And the heart of education is experimentation—we learn by doing. This learning is an achieving that never fully achieves. There will always be room for more human progress. There will never be a millennium, only a

36. Ibid., p. 26.
37. Ibid., pp. 38 – 39.

continual and relative process of seeking new goals by means of pragmatic experimentation.

There are three broad areas in which Dewey's humanism will be evaluated here: its pragmatism, progressivism, and relativism. Other aspects such as naturalism and educational philosophy will be left for another time.

Pragmatism

Dewey's pragmatism is manifest on two important levels: truth and ethics. The pragmatic view of truth is that whatever works is true. This, however, is an insufficient view of truth. For many things that work very well (such as lies) are false. Truth is not what works but what corresponds with the facts.[38] No pragmatist would appreciate someone's misrepresenting his view simply because it worked well to do so. Pragmatists or not, parents do not want their child to lie to them simply because it is helpful or expedient for the child to do so. One is reminded in this connection of Josiah Royce's famous criticism of pragmatism: he wondered whether William James, a leading exponent of pragmatism, would be willing to take the witness stand in court and swear to tell the expedient, the whole expedient, and nothing but the expedient, so help him future experience!

Pragmatism fares no better in the realm of ethics.[39] Not everything that works is right. Some things that work very well are simply evil. Cheating, deceiving, and even killing undesirables are only a few of man's successful but evil activities. Even when something succeeds we can still ask whether it is *right*, for the ethical question of right or wrong is not settled by obtaining the desired results; desired results can be wrong. Actually, all that "success" proves is that that course of action *worked;* it does not prove that it was *right.*

Progressivism

Actually Dewey's relativism is not total. He has a kind of absolute in his system: progress or achievement. Whatever works for social

---

38. See a defense of the "correspondence" view of truth in Norman L. Geisler, "The Concept of Truth in the Inerrancy Debate," *Bibliotheca Sacra* (October-December, 1980), pp. 332 – 339.

39. See Geisler, *Introduction to Philosophy: A Christian Perspective* (Grand Rapids: Baker, 1980), pp. 393 – 394.

progress is good, and what hinders it is evil. This view, however, has several problems. First, by what standard does one judge the progress of mankind? If the standard is within society then we cannot be sure we are progressing. Maybe we are really only changing, not progressing. If, on the other hand, the standard is outside society, we have a transcendent norm—a kind of divine imperative—which Dewey rejects.[40]

Another problem with progressivism is that everything cannot be changing. There must be some fixed point by which one measures change or progress. Otherwise one could not even measure the change. If, for example, an observer of a moving car is in a moving car himself, he cannot know how fast the other car is moving. And if the other car is moving at the same speed, then the observer cannot even know it is moving unless he has some stationary object by which to judge that the other car is moving.

One final note on Dewey's progressivism. Why *social* progressivism? In fact, why *democratic* social progressivism? There are other ways to "progress." One can move toward socialistic or communistic goals too. One could even progress toward better dictatorships! Dewey's definition of achievement or progress in social and democratic terms is philosophically unjustified. It stands on no better ground than other goals one may choose. It is in fact arbitrary to insist that democratic "achievement" is the only kind of progress to press for. Even many other humanists, Marxists and existentialists among them, would disagree.

Relativism

Closely allied to progressivism is relativism. Dewey denies absolutes in the realm of truth or ethics. But this is inconsistent. For to show that *all* is relative one must have a nonrelative vantage point from which to view all. One cannot say that all else is relative unless he stands on absolute ground. The very statement "all is relative" either includes itself or it does not. If it includes itself than it is self-defeating. If it does not include itself then it makes itself a special case. Everything else is relative; it alone is absolute! But this would be pure dogmatism.

40. See C. S. Lewis, *Mere Christianity* (New York: Macmillan, 1943), pp. 24 – 26.

5

Marxist Humanism

Judged by the standard of political influence, Marxism is the most widespread form of humanism in the world. Its founder, Karl Marx, was born in 1818 to a German Jewish family which was converted to Lutheranism when he was six. As a university student he was influenced heavily by Georg Hegel's idealism, and he adopted Ludwig Feuerbach's atheism. After some radical political activity, which resulted in expulsion from France in 1845, he teamed up with Friedrich Engels to produce the *Communist Manifesto* (1848). With the economic support of Engels's prosperous textile business Marx spent years of research in the British Museum and produced his famous *Das Kapital* (1867). These and succeeding Marxist writings have bequeathed a form of humanistic thought that is politically dominant in much of the world.

The Marxist View of God and Religion

Even as a college student Marx was a militant atheist who believed that the "criticism of religion is the foundation of all criticism." For this criticism Marx drew heavily on the radical young Hegelian, Ludwig Feuerbach. Engels admitted that Feuerbach influenced them more than did any other post-Hegelian philosopher.[1] He triumphantly spoke of Feuerbach's *Essence of Christianity* which "with

1. See *Marx and Engels on Religion*, ed. Reinhold Niebuhr (New York: Schocken, 1964), p. 214.

one blow ... pulverized [religion] ... in that without circumlocution it placed materialism on the throne again."[2]

There were three basic premises Marx learned from Feuerbach. First, "the teaching that man is the highest essence for man"[3] was accepted. This means that there is a categorical imperative to overthrow anything—especially religion—which debases man. Secondly, Marx accepted the premise of Feuerbach that "man makes religion, religion does not make man."[4] In other words, religion is the self-consciousness of man who has lost himself and then found himself again as "God." Thirdly, Marx also accepted the Feuerbachian belief that "all religion ... is nothing but the fantastic reflection in men's minds of those external forces which control their daily life, a reflection in which the terrestrial forces assume the form of supernatural forces."[5] In brief, God is nothing but a projection of human imagination. God did not make man in His image; man has made "God" in his image.

Marx's atheism, however, went well beyond Feuerbach. Marx agreed with the materialists that "matter is not a product of mind, but mind itself is merely the highest product of matter."[6] That is, he agreed with Feuerbach that man in seeking his origin must look backward to pure matter. Marx, however, objected that Feuerbach did not go forward in the social domain. For Feuerbach by no means wished to abolish religion; he wanted to perfect it.[7] Feuerbach, reasoned Marx, did not see that the "religious sentiment" is itself a social product.[8] Hence "he [did] not grasp the significance of 'revolutionary,' of 'practical-critical,' activity."[9] Feuerbach did not realize, in the words of Marxism's famous slogan, that "religion is the opium of the people."[10] Man needs to take the drug of religion because this world is not adequate to assure him of his complete and integrated development. So he compensates himself with the image of another, more perfect world.[11]

2. Ibid., p. 224.
3. Ibid., p. 50.
4. Ibid., p. 41.
5. Ibid., p. 147.
6. Ibid., p. 231.
7. Ibid., p. 237.
8. Ibid., p. 71.
9. Ibid., p. 69.
10. Ibid., p. 35.
11. Ibid., p. 36.

In going beyond Feuerbach, Marx argued that "nowadays, in our evolutionary conception of the universe, there is absolutely no room for either a Creator or a Ruler; and to talk of a Supreme Being shut out from the whole existing world [as deism does] implies a contradiction in terms."[12] Hence, concluded Marx, "the only service that can be rendered to God today is to declare atheism a compulsory article of faith and . . . [to prohibit] religion generally."[13]

Marx had no illusions that religion would immediately cease to exist when socialism was adopted. Since religion is but a reflex of the real world, religion will not vanish until the practical relations of everyday life offer to man perfect relations with regard to his fellow men and to nature[14]—that is, until the communist utopia is realized.

The Marxist View of Man

Basically Marxism holds a materialistic view of man's origin and nature. This, of course, entails an evolutionary concept of man's origin.

The Origin of Man

Darwin's *Origin of Species* was published in 1859. Marx's *Das Kapital* came out only eight years later (in 1867). Evolution for Marx was a helpful addition to his materialistic understanding of the origin of man. "Mind is the product of matter," he wrote; that is, mind has evolved from material stuff. The nonliving matter has always been; it has produced the living, and finally, the nonintelligent has produced the intelligent (man).

Marx had written his doctoral thesis (at the University of Jena, 1841) on the materialistic philosophies of two early Greek philosophers, Epicurus and Democritus. Then with the subsequent support of Darwinian evolution he could explain the origin of human life as

12. Ibid., p. 295. Even agnosticism was rejected by Marx: "What, indeed, is agnosticism but, to use an expressive Lancashire term, 'shamefaced' materialism? The agnostic conception of nature is materialistic throughout."
13. Ibid., p. 143.
14. Ibid., p. 136.

the product of evolutionary processes in a material world—there was no longer any need to speak of God.

The Nature of Man

Marx was not interested in pure philosophy, which he dismissed as mere speculation and quite useless when compared to the vital task of changing the world.[15] Hence he was not particularly interested in philosophical materialism. His being designated a materialist, however, does not mean that he denied mind altogether (as he denied life after death). Rather he believed that everything about man, including his mind, is determined by his material conditions. "For us," said Marx, "mind is a mode of energy, a function of brain; all we know is that the material world is governed by immutable laws, and so forth."[16] This view would fit with what philosophers call epiphenomenalism, according to which consciousness is nonmaterial but dependent on material things for its existence.

Karl Marx was more interested in man in the concrete, in man as a social being. He believed that "the real nature of man is the total of *social* nature."[17] Apart from the obvious biological facts such as man's need for food, Marx tended to downplay individual human existence. He believed that what is true of one man at one time in one society is also true of all men at all times in all places.[18] Thus "it is not [that] the consciousness of men ... determines their being, but ... their social being determines their consciousness."[19] In short, psychology is reducible to sociology, but sociology is not reducible to psychology.

One important generalization Marx makes about human nature is that man is a socially active being who distinguishes himself from other animals in that he *produces* his means of subsistence.[20] That is, it is natural for men to work for their living. Thus, Marx concludes, it is *right* for men to have a life of productive activity, to be workers.

15. See Marx, *Selected Writings in Sociology and Social Philosophy*, trans. T. B. Bottomore (New York: McGraw-Hill, 1964), p. 82.
16. *Marx and Engels on Religion*, p. 298.
17. Marx, *Selected Writings*, p. 83.
18. Ibid., pp. 91 – 92.
19. Ibid., p. 67.
20. Ibid., p. 69.

The Alienation of Man

Men who do not find fulfillment in industrial labor will experience
alienation. This alienation will be eliminated when private property
is done away with.[21] Private property, however, is not the cause but
a consequence of alienation.[22] The alienation itself consists in the
fact that the work is not part of the worker's nature. He is not fulfilled
in work because it is forced on him so that someone else may be
fulfilled. Even the objects he produces are alien to him because they
are owned by another. The cure for this ill will be the future communist society in which everyone can cultivate his talent by working
for the good of the whole commune of mankind.[23] It is in this sense
that Marxism is appropriately called a humanism.

The Marxist View of the World and History

The Dialectic of History

As has been noted already, Marx's overall view of the world is
materialistic. He uses the term *historical materialism* "to designate
that view of the course of history which seeks the ultimate cause
and the great moving power of all important historic events in the
economic development of society."[24] Further, Marx can be classified
as a *dialectical* materialist, following in the tradition of the Hegelian
dialectic of thesis, antithesis, and synthesis.[25] History is unfolding
according to a universal dialectical law the outworking of which can
be predicted the way an astronomer predicts an eclipse. In the preface to *Das Kapital* Marx compares his method to that of a physicist:
"The ultimate aim of this work is to lay bare the economic law of
motion of modern society." He also speaks of the natural laws of

21. Ibid., p. 250.
22. Ibid., p. 176.
23. Ibid., pp. 177, 253.
24. *Marx and Engels on Religion*, p. 298.
25. Hegel himself rejected this dialectic, though it is commonly attributed to
him. See Gustav E. Mueller, "The Hegel Legend of Thesis-Antithesis-Synthesis," *Journal of the History of Ideas* 19, no. 3 (1958): 411 – 414.

capitalistic production as "working with iron necessity toward inevitable results."[26]

The dialectic of modern history is that the thesis of capitalism is opposed by the antithesis of socialism, which will unavoidably give way to the ultimate synthesis of communism. History is predetermined like the course of the stars, except that the laws governing history are not mechanical but economic in nature. Man is economically determined. That is, "the mode of production of material life determines the general character of the social, political, and spiritual processes of life."[27] This, of course, does not mean that man is determined *solely* by economic factors. Marx means only that the economic is the primary or dominant influence on man's social character. Engels emphatically proclaimed, "More than this neither Marx nor I have ever asserted. Hence if somebody twists this into saying that the economic element is the *only* determining one, he transforms that proposition into a meaningless, abstract, senseless phrase."[28]

The Future of Capitalism

On the basis of his assumption that the dialectic of history is carried out by means of economic determinism, Marx confidently predicted that capitalism would become increasingly unstable and that the class struggle between the bourgeoisie (ruling class) and the proletariat (working class) would intensify. The poor would become larger and poorer until, by a major social revolution, they would seize power and institute the new communist phase of history.[29]

The fact that these predictions did not come to pass remains an embarrassment to Marxist theory. It casts doubt on the scientific and predictive value of orthodox Marxism.

The Future Communistic Utopia

According to Marx, capitalism has internal problems which will eventually lead to a communistic economic system. For as the masses

26. *Das Kapital*, ed. Friedrich Engels, trans. Samuel Moore and Edward Aveling, in Great Books of the Western World, ed. Robert Maynard Hutchins (Chicago: Encyclopedia Britannica, 1952), vol. 50, p. 6.
27. Marx, *Selected Writings*, p. 67; cf. pp. 70, 90, 111ff.
28. *Marx and Engels on Religion*, p. 274.
29. See Marx, *Selected Writings*, pp. 79 – 80, 147ff., 236.

become more numerous and the capitalists fewer, the latter will control great concentrations of productive equipment which they will throttle for their own gain. But the masses will then sweep aside the capitalists as a hindrance to production and seize an industrial economy which has been carried to the edge of perfection by self-liquidating capitalism. Thus there will emerge a progressive society with no wages, no money, no social classes, and eventually no state. This communist utopia will simply be a free association of producers under their own conscious control. Society will ultimately realize the communist ideal: "From each according to his ability, to each according to his need."[30] There will, however, be the need for an intermediate period of "the dictatorship of the proletariat."[31] But in the higher stage the state will vanish and true freedom will begin.

The Marxist Ethic

There are several characteristic dimensions of the ethics of Marxism. Three of these are relativism, utilitarianism, and collectivism.

Relativism

Since Marxism is atheistic, and since, as Nietzsche noted, when God dies all absolute value dies with Him, it is understandable that Marxist ethics is relativistic. That is, there are no moral absolutes. There are two reasons for this. First, there is no external, eternal realm. The only absolute is the inexorable progress of the unfolding dialectic of history. Engels wrote, "We therefore reject every attempt to impose on us any moral dogma whatever as an eternal, ultimate and forever immutable law on the pretext that the moral world has its permanent principles which transcend history."[32]

Secondly, there is no such thing as a nature or essence of man which could serve as a foundation for general principles of human conduct. Man's ideas of good and evil are determined by man's con-

30. Ibid., p. 263.
31. Ibid., p. 261.
32. Quoted in R. N. Carew Hunt, *The Theory and Practice of Communism* (New York: Macmillan, 1962), pp. 87 – 88.

crete place in the socioeconomic structure. In brief, class struggle generates its own ethic.

Utilitarianism

On what basis are one's actions regarded as moral? The answer is, they are regarded as moral if they serve to create a new communist society. Actions can be justified by their end. Lenin once defined morality as that which serves to destroy the exploiting capitalistic society and to unite workers in creating a new communist society,[33] in effect saying that the end justifies the means.[34] This is the communist's equivalent of utilitarianism's "greatest good for the greatest number in the long run." Whatever promotes the ultimate cause of communism is good, and what hinders it is evil.

Collectivism

Another feature of Marxist ethics is that the universal transcends the individual. This is a heritage from Hegel, who believed that the perfect life is possible only when the individual is organically integrated into the ethical totality. For Marx, however, the highest ethical totality is not the state (as it was for Hegel) but "universal freedom of will." Note that this "freedom" is not individual but corporate and universal. The difference from Hegel is that the emphasis is shifted from the state to society, from the body politic to the body public.

According to Marx, in the perfect society private morals are eliminated and the ethical ideals of the community are achieved. This will be accomplished, of course, by material production. For material production determines religion, metaphysics, and morality.[35]

An Evaluation of Marxist Humanism

Several aspects of Marxism call for comment here. Some comments will be of a positive nature; a large number, however, will point out weaknesses in Marx's philosophy.

33. Ibid., p. 89.

34. Some neo-Marxists have rejected this, insisting that means are subject to the same moral principles as the end. But they have thereby departed from orthodox Marxism. See George H. Hampsch, *The Theory of Communism* (Secaucus, N. J.: Citadel, 1965), p. 127.

35. See Marx, *The Communist Manifesto*, ed. Samuel H. Beer (New York: Appleton-Century-Crofts, 1955), p. 177.

Positive Contributions of Marxism

Marx's concern for the condition of workers is to be commended. Working conditions are vastly improved today from those of over a century ago when Marx wrote. Likewise, Marx is certainly right in attacking the view that workers are merely a means to the end of capitalistic gain. Thus there has been a significant humanistic contribution in that Marxist philosophy places man over money.

Another positive contribution of Marxism has been its corrective on unlimited and uncontrolled capitalism. Any system which permits the rich to get richer and makes the poor poorer without limits is bound to produce ethical abuses. In the ancient Jewish economy this possibility was checked by the Year of Jubilee (every fiftieth year), when acquisitions were returned to their original owners.[36]

Finally, the millennial aspirations of Marxism are noble. Indeed, the Marxist philosophy of history encourages men to work toward the goal of overcoming the perceived evils of the present world. It is this humanistic vision which has captured the imagination and dedication of many young thinkers.

Negative Features of Marxism

Marxism is subject to numerous critiques. We will briefly indicate some of the more significant ones.

First, the dogmatic atheism of Marxism is unfounded. It is self-defeating to insist that God is nothing but a projection of human imagination. "Nothing but" statements presume "more than" knowledge. One cannot know that God is confined to imagination unless one's knowledge goes beyond mere imagination.

Second, Marx's deterministic view of history is ill founded. Not only is it contrary to fact—since things have not worked out as Marx predicted—but it is a category mistake to assume that economic influence works like physical laws.

Third, a materialistic view of man ignores the rich spiritual and religious aspects of human nature, to say nothing of the evidence for man's immateriality and immortality.

Fourth, in its strongest form ethical relativism is self-destructive. The absolute denial of absolutes cuts its own throat. And to replace

36. Lev. 25.

one absolute with another (the communist end) does not avoid absolutism. Also, the fallacies of the "end justifies the means" ethic are infamous.

Fifth, Marxism holds out an admirably idealistic goal (a human utopia) but has a miserable record of achievement. Life in Marxist countries has been more like hell than heaven. While the goal of a perfect community is desirable, the revolutionary means of achieving it is highly questionable. From a Christian perspective the means of transforming mankind is not revolution but regeneration. It begins not with the birth of a new government but with the birth of a new man—that is, the new birth (John 3:5).

Sixth, Marx's view of religion is superficial. He should have heeded his father's exhortation to him at age seventeen: "Faith [in God] is a real [requirement] of man sooner or later, and there are moments in life when even the atheist is [involuntarily] drawn to worship the Almighty."[37] Or better yet, in view of his later tumultuous life and the revolutions his thought has precipitated in the world, Marx should have applied his own earlier thoughts: "Union with Christ bestows inner exaltation, consolation in suffering, calm assurance, and a heart which is open to love of mankind, to all that is noble, to all that is great, not out of ambition, not through the desire of fame, but only because of Christ."[38]

Karl Marx's own father feared it was the desire for fame which transformed Karl's Christian conscience into a demonic passion. In March 1837 he admonished his ambitious son:

> From time to time, my heart revels in the thoughts of you and your future. And yet, from time to time, I cannot escape the sad, suspicious, fearful thoughts that strike like lightning: Does your heart match your head and your talents? Does it have room for the earthly but gentler feelings that are such an essential consolation to the sensitive human being in this vale of sorrows? Is the demon, which is clearly not given to or dominated by everybody, of a celestial or a Faustian nature?[39]

37. Letter from Trier, November 18, 1835.
38. Written by Marx between August 10 and 16, 1835.
39. Saul K. Padover, *Karl Marx: An Intimate Biography* (New York: McGraw-Hill, 1978), p. 97.

Egocentric Humanism

Marxism is a collectivistic form of humanism. In stark contrast to this is the individualistic humanism of the American novelist Ayn Rand. The former advocates communism, and the latter defends capitalism. Rand's egocentric humanism also stands in contrast to the existential humanism of Jean-Paul Sartre. Sartre stresses the subjective and nonrational; Rand emphasizes the objective and rational.

The Atheistic Element

Rand is an atheistic humanist. For her, "matter is indestructible; it changes its forms, but it cannot cease to exist." But if "the existence of inanimate matter is unconditional, the existence of life is not." For "life is a process of self-sustaining and self-generating action." This means that "if an organism fails in that action, it dies; its chemical elements remain, but its life goes out of existence."[1] In short, life came to be (by evolution) and it can cease to be; matter ever was and ever will be.

Whence, then, came the idea of "God"? Rand answers, "Faith in the supernatural begins as faith in the superiority of others."[2] Faith is, as Freud said, an illusion. "The secret of all their esoteric philosophies, of all their dialectics and super-senses, ... is erect upon that plastic fog, a single holy absolute: their Wish."[3] But, continues Rand, "those irrational wishes that draw you to their creed, those emotions

---

1. Ayn Rand, *The Virtue of Selfishness* (New York: Signet, 1964), p. 15.
2. Rand, *For the New Intellectual* (New York: Signet, 1961), p. 161.
3. Ibid., p. 149.

you worship as an idol . . . which you take as the voice of God or of your glands, [are] nothing more than the corpse of your mind."[4]

According to Rand, "when a mystic declares that he feels the existence of a power superior to reason, he feels it all right, but that power is not an omniscient super spirit of the universe, it is the consciousness of any passer-by to whom he has surrendered his own."[5] Such surrender to others is, of course, contrary to the ego-centric philosophy of Rand, who sees the individual as ultimate. Her view of God is expressed by the hero of the novel *Atlas Shrugged:* "And now I see the face of god, and I raise this god over the earth, this god whom men have sought since men came into being, this god who will grant them joy and peace and pride. This god, this one word: I."[6]

Since no God created man, he does not belong to another but to himself. Rand bemoans the fact that "for centuries, the battle for morality was fought between those who claimed that your life belongs to God and those who claimed that it belongs to your neighbors. . . . And no one came to say that your life belongs to you and that it is good to live it."[7] This situation Rand attempts to correct by affirming that "by the grace of reality and nature of life, man—every man—is an end in himself, he exists for his own sake, and the achievement of his own happiness is his highest moral purpose."[8]

The Nature and Purpose of Man

While traditional Christians have defined the chief end of man as glorifying God and enjoying Him forever, Rand boldly proclaims that man's chief end is himself and his own happiness. But before we can fully understand man's purpose it will be helpful to know more about his nature.

Man Is More than Material

Rand rejects strict materialism. Man is more than mere matter. In fact, man is more than mere animal life. Man has a unique ability

4. Ibid., p. 151.
5. Ibid., p. 161.
6. Quoted in Rand, *New Intellectual*, p. 65.
7. Ibid., p. 120.
8. Ibid., p. 123.

not shared by animals: the ability to reason. As Aristotle said, man is a rational animal. And along with reason man has volition. In Rand's words,

> Man's consciousness shares with animals the first two stages of its development: sensations and perceptions; but it is the third state, *conceptions*, that makes him man. Sensations are integrated into perceptions automatically, by the brain of a man or of an animal. But to integrate perceptions into conceptions by a process of abstraction, is a feat that man alone has the power to perform—and he has to perform it *by choice.*[9]

Man Is Rational

Thus "man is the only living species who has to perceive reality—which means: to be *conscious*—by choice."[10] And man is the only conscious being that can conceptualize. Conceptualization is not merely a passive registering of random impressions. It is an actively sustained process of identifying one's impressions in conceptual terms, of grasping relationships, or integration, and of rational inferences. "The faculty that directs this process ... is: *reason*. The process is *thinking*."[11]

Although Rand believes that men are born a *tabula rasa* (blank slate) and learn through their senses, she rejects the strict empiricism of David Hume:

> If it were possible for an animal to describe the content of his consciousness, the result would be a transcript of Hume's philosophy. Hume's conclusions would be the conclusions of a consciousness limited to the perceptual level of awareness, passively reacting to the experience of immediate concretes, with no capacity to form abstractions, to *integrate* perceptions into concepts, waiting in vain for the appearance of an object labeled "causality" (except that such a consciousness would not be able to draw conclusions).[12]

It is not so with man, for he is eminently a reasoning being. Reason is man's guardian and his means of survival. "For man, the basic

9. Ibid., p. 14.
10. Ibid., p. 5.
11. Rand, *Virtue*, p. 20.
12. Rand, *New Intellectual*, p. 29.

means of survival is *reason*. Man cannot survive, as animals do, by the guidance of mere precepts." For instance, "a sensation of hunger will tell him that he needs food ... but it will not tell him how to obtain his food."[13] No instinct will tell man how to build a fire. Hence "man has no automatic code of survival. He has no automatic course of action, no automatic set of values."[14]

> Man cannot survive except through his mind. He comes on earth unarmed. His brain is his only weapon. Animals obtain food by force. Man has no claws, no fangs, no horns, no great strength of muscle. He must plant his food or hunt it. To plant, he needs a process of thought. To hunt, he needs weapons, and to make weapons—a process of thought. From this simplest necessity to the highest religious abstraction, from the wheel to the skyscraper, everything we are and everything we have comes from a single attribute of man—the function of his reasoning mind.[15]

Further, "your mind is your only judge of truth—and if others dissent from your verdict, reality is the court of final appeal." Hence "truth is the recognition of reality: reason, man's only means of knowledge, is his only standard of truth."[16]

Man Is Volitional

Since man cannot even survive on purely animal instinct level without using his reason to make rational choices, "man's particular distinction from all other living species is the fact that *his* consciousness is *volitional*."[17] Hence

> man has been called a rational being, but rationality is a matter of choice—and the alternative his nature offers him is: rational being or suicidal animal. Man has to be man—by choice; he has to hold his life as a value—by choice; he has to learn to sustain it—by choice; he has to discover the values it requires and practice his virtues—by choice. A code of values accepted by choice is a code of morality.[18]

13. Rand, *Virtue*, p. 21.
14. Rand, *New Intellectual*, p. 19.
15. Ibid., p. 78.
16. Ibid., p. 126.
17. Ibid., p. 20.
18. Ibid., p. 23.

By contrast "an animal has no choice in the knowledge and the skills that it acquires." And "an animal has no choice in the standard of value directing its actions: its senses provide it with an *automatic* code of values, an automatic knowledge of what is good for it or evil."[19] Not so with man: he must choose his own means to happiness.

Man Is Not Inherently Sinful

Rand is vehemently opposed to the Christian doctrine of original sin:

> The name of this monstrous absurdity is Original Sin. A sin without volition is a slap at morality and an insolent contradiction in terms: that which is outside the possibility of choice is outside the province of morality. If man is evil by birth, he has no will, no power to change it; if he has no will, he can be neither good nor evil: a robot is amoral. To hold, as man's sin, a fact not open to his voice is a mockery of morality. To hold man's nature as his sin is a mockery of nature. To punish him for a crime he committed before he was born is a mockery of justice. To hold him guilty in a matter where no innocence exists is a mockery of reason.[20]

Furthermore, Rand considers it a "cowardly evasion" to believe "that man is born with a free will, but with a 'tendency' to do evil." For

> a free will saddled with a tendency is like a game with loaded dice, it forces man to struggle through the effort of playing, to bear responsibility and pay for the game but the decision is weighted in favor of a tendency that he has no power to escape. If the tendency is of his choice, he cannot possess it at birth; if it is not of his choice, his will is not free.[21]

Man Is Mortal

Rand does not wish to speculate on life beyond this mortal existence. She declares, "I know not if this earth on which I stand is the core of the universe or if it is but a speck of dust lost in eternity. I

19. Ibid., p. 19.
20. Ibid., pp. 136 – 137.
21. Ibid., p. 137.

know not and I care not." For "I know what happiness is possible to me on earth. And my happiness needs no higher aim to vindicate it. My happiness is not the means to any end. It is the end. It is its own goal. It is its own purpose."[22]

Man Is an Individual

Perhaps more than almost anything else Rand insists that man is an individual. So strongly is she opposed to a collectivistic concept of man that she views the word *we* as an evil word. "It is the word by which the depraved steal the virtue from the good, by which the weak steal the might of the strong, by which the fools steal the wisdom of the ages." Hence "the word 'We' must never be spoken, save by one's choice and as a second thought. This word must never be placed first within man's soul, else it becomes a monster, the root of all the evils on earth, the root of man's torture by men, and of an unspeakable lie."[23]

In the same vein Rand claims that "the mind is an attribute of the individual. There is no such thing as a collective brain."[24] Hence "no work is ever done collectively, by a majority decision. Every creative job is achieved under the guidance of a single individual thought."[25] Man must be understood as *individual* man.

The Norm for Man's Conduct

There is no divine basis for ethics. God does not exist; therefore man is responsible to and for himself. To repeat, "man—every man— is an end in himself, he exists for his own sake."[26] This does not mean, however, that man can do anything he chooses to do.

Objectivity

Rand in fact decries ethical subjectivism: "If you wonder why the world is now collapsing to a lower and ever lower rung of hell, *this*

22. Ibid., p. 64.
23. Ibid., p. 65.
24. Ibid., p. 79.
25. Ibid., p. 82.
26. Ibid., p. 123.

is the reason."[27] Rand rejects this "whim" ethic, calling it "arbitrary," "subjective," and a mere "emotional commitment." Virtually everyone seems to hold this subjective kind of ethic today, writes Rand. "The battle is only over the question of *whose* whim: one's own or society's or the dictator's or God's."[28]

In contrast with this prevailing subjectivism Rand offers her own "objectivist ethics." By this she means "rational selfishness" or the values required for man's survival as man. This in contrast to "values produced by the desires, the emotions, the aspirations, the feelings, the whims or the needs of irrational brutes, who have never outgrown the primordial practices of human sacrifices."[29]

In summation, "ethics is *not* a mystic fantasy—nor a social convention—nor a dispensable, subjective luxury, to be switched or discarded in any emergency." Rather, "ethics is an *objective, metaphysical necessity* of man's survival."[30]

Man-Centeredness

The heart of Rand's humanism is its egocentricity. Man—individual man—is the ultimate norm for himself. For "the Objectivist ethic holds man's life as the *standard* of value—and *his own life* as the ethical purpose of every individual man."[31] As such, one's life is the ultimate value. "No value is higher than self-esteem." In fact, man "has no choice about his need for self-esteem, his only choice is the standard by which to gauge it."[32] Hence "the first right on earth is the right of the ego. Man's first duty is to himself."[33]

What obligation does a man have to others? "None—except the obligation I owe to myself, to material objects and to all of existence: rationality." That is to say, "I deal with men as my nature and theirs demands: my means of reason. . . . It is only with their mind that I can deal and only for my own self-interest."[34]

In brief, man is an end in himself. He exists for himself and not

27. Rand, *Virtue,* p. 15.
28. Ibid., p. 15.
29. Ibid., p. 31.
30. Ibid., p. 23.
31. Ibid., p. 25.
32. Rand, *New Intellectual,* p. 176.
33. Ibid., p. 82.
34. Ibid., p. 133.

for others. Hence self-love is the most basic duty of all. In fact, loving others (as one may choose to do) is possible only for a selfish man. For "to love is to value. Only a rationally selfish man, a man of self-esteem, is capable of love. . . . The man who does not value himself, cannot value anything or anyone."[35]

For those who would challenge this philosophy of selfishness Rand asks, "Why is it immoral to produce a value and keep it, but moral to give it away? And if it is not moral for you to keep a value, why is it moral for others to accept it? If you are selfless and virtuous when you give it, are they not selfish and vicious when they take it?"[36]

Trade Orientation

Rand is an uncompromising capitalist. The profit motive is paramount in all dealings with others. Hence one should love others only if there is some "profit" in it for himself. We should love only those who are worthy of our love. "To love those who are worthy of it is self-interest; to love the unworthy is sacrifice." And to love the unworthy is "a blank check on vice."[37] But is there ever a moral duty to help another? "No—if he claims it as his right or as a moral *duty* that you owe him." One has a moral duty to help another only "if such is your own *desire* based on your own selfish pleasure in the value of his person and his struggle."[38]

Virtues should never be given away as a duty; they should be traded. "If you choose to help a man who suffers, do it only on the ground of his virtues, . . . then your action is still a trade, and his virtue is the payment for your help." But simply "to help a man who has no virtues, to help him on the ground of his suffering as such, to accept his faults, his need, as a claim—is to accept the mortgage of a zero on your values."[39] Rand says, "I do not grant my love without reason, nor to any chance passer-by who may wish to claim it. I honor men with my love. But honor is a thing to be earned."[40]

35. Rand, *Virtue*, p. 32.
36. Rand, *New Intellectual*, p. 144.
37. Rand, *Virtue*, p. 147.
38. Rand, *New Intellectual*, p. 180 (emphasis added).
39. Ibid., p. 180.
40. Ibid., p. 65.

Hence

> the creed of sacrifice is a morality for the immoral—a morality that
> declares its own bankruptcy by confessing that it can't impart to men
> any personal stake in virtues or values, and that their souls are sewers
> of depravity, which they must be taught to sacrifice. By its own confes-
> sion, it is impotent to teach men to be good and can only subject
> them to constant punishment.[41]

Basic Ethical Values

According to Rand, "*value* is that which one acts to gain and/or
keep—*virtue* is the act by which one gains and/or keeps it." And "the
three cardinal values of the Objectivist ethics are: Reason, Purpose,
Self-esteem, with their corresponding virtues: Rationality, Productiv-
ity, Pride."[42] Man needs "Reason, as his only tool of knowledge—
Purpose, as his choice of the happiness which that tool must proceed to achieve—Self-esteem, as his inviolate certainty that his mind
is competent to think and his person is worthy of happiness, which
means: is worthy of living."[43]

Man's most basic right is the "right to his own life . . . which means:
man's right to exist for his own sake."[44] In this pursuit of his own
good "man's only moral commandment is: Thou shalt think." But
Rand hastens to add that "the moral is the chosen, not the forced;
the understood, not the obeyed." For "the moral is the rational, and
reason accepts no commandments."[45] So in reality "man has a single
basic choice: to think or not, and that is the gauge of his virtue. Moral
perfection is an *unbreached rationality*, . . . the acceptance of reason
as an absolute."[46]

The Social Goal: Pure Capitalism

Rand, like most humanists, is a utopian. And, like Marx, Rand is
convinced that the desired millennium is economically determined.
However, here the essential similarities stop. For Marx is a commu-

41. Ibid., p. 141.
42. Rand, *Virtue*, p. 25.
43. Rand, *New Intellectual*, p. 128.
44. Ibid., p. 53.
45. Ibid., p. 128.
46. Ibid., pp. 178 – 179.

nist, and Rand a capitalist. Marx is a collectivist; Rand is an individualist.

The Evil of Socialism

Even the word *we* is evil for Rand. No work is ever accomplished by a group. "There is no such thing as a collective brain."[47] Rand chides, "We've found the magic word. Collectivism. Look at Europe, you fool. . . . The individual held as evil, the mass—as God."[48]

"Collectivism," says Rand, "is dead, but capitalism has not yet been discovered."[49] And it is good that collectivism is a defunct ideology, for it "was the claim and justification of every tyranny ever established over men. Every major horror in history was committed in the name of an altruistic motive. . . . Nobody questioned [tyrants'] right to murder since they were murdering for an altruistic purpose."[50] Rand detests "the *moral cannibalism* of all hedonist and altruist doctrines [which] lies in the premise that the happiness of one man necessitates the injury of another."[51]

"The only proper purpose of a government is to protect Man's rights, which means: to protect him from physical violence." That is, "a proper government is only a policeman, acting as an agent of man's self-defense, and, as such, may resort to force only against those who start the use of force." Hence "the only proper functions of a government are: the police, to protect you from criminals; the army, to protect you from foreign invaders; and the courts, to protect your property and contracts from breach or fraud by others, to settle disputes by rational rules, according to objective law."[52] Therefore "so long as men desire to live together, no man may initiate—do you hear me? no man may start—the use of physical force against others."[53]

Capitalism: The Greatest Good

The ideal human society, then, is one with the minimum of government and the maximum of capitalistic activity. "Capitalism

47. Ibid., p. 79.
48. Ibid., p. 76.
49. Ibid., p. 46.
50. Ibid., p. 83.
51. Rand, *Virtue*, p. 30.
52. Rand, *New Intellectual*, p. 183.
53. Ibid., p. 134.

demands the best of every man—his rationality—and rewards him accordingly." Under capitalism a man's "success depends on the *objective* value of his work and on the rationality of those who recognize that value." According to Rand, "capitalism wiped out slavery in matter and in spirit."[54] And capitalism is capable of solving conflicts of interest in society. For "there is no conflict of interest among men who do not desire the unearned, . . . who deal with one another as *traders*, giving value for value." Hence "the principle of *trade* is the only rational principle for all human relationships, personal and social, private and public, spiritual and material. It is the principle of *justice.*"[55]

The ideal society is one where there is no irrational illusion of causeless wealth; everything has a cause. And just "as there can be no causeless wealth, so there can be no causeless love or any sort of causeless emotion. An emotion is a response to a fact of reality, an estimate dictated by your standards. To love is to value." So then, "the man who tells you that it is possible to value without values, to love those whom you appraise as worthless, is the man who tells you that it is possible to grow rich by consuming without producing and that paper money is as valuable as gold."[56]

To those who would point to the failures of capitalism to achieve its utopian goals, Rand replies, "When they hear it said that capitalism has had its chance and has failed, let them remember that what ultimately failed was a 'mixed' economy, that the controls were the cause of the failure, and that the way to save a country is not by making it swallow a full, 'unmixed' glass of the poison which is killing it."[57] Indeed, "if [capitalism] perishes, it will perish by default, undiscovered and unidentified: no other subject has ever been hidden by so many distortions, misconceptions and misrepresentations. Today, few people know what capitalism is, how it works and what was its actual history."[58]

The Need for New Intellectuals

In order to achieve these capitalistic and humanistic goals, Rand calls for a special breed of man: "the new intellectual." He "will be

54. Ibid., p. 25.
55. Rand, *Virtue*, p. 31.
56. Rand, *New Intellectual*, p. 147.
57. Ibid., p. 53.
58. Rand, *Virtue*, p. 33.

the man who lives up to the exact meaning of his title: a man who is guided by his *intellect*—not a zombie guided by feelings, instincts, urges, wishes, whims or revelations."[59] The new intellectual

> will discard ... irrational conflicts and contradictions, such as: mind *versus* heart, thought *versus* action, reality *versus* desire, the practical *versus* the moral. He will be an *integrated man*, that is: a thinker who is a man of action. He will know that ideas divorced from consequent action are fraudulent, and that action divorced from ideas is suicidal.[60]

To put it on a practical level,

> there ought to be a private, voluntary program of "student exchanges" between the intellectuals and the businessmen, the two groups that need each other most, yet know less and understand less about each other than about any alien society in any distant corner of the globe. The businessmen need to discover the intellect; the intellectuals need to discover reality. Let the intellectuals understand the nature and the function of a free market in order to offer the businessmen, as well as the public at large, the guidance of an intelligible theoretical framework for dealing with men, with society, with politics, with economics. Let the businessmen learn the basic issues and principles of philosophy in order to know how to judge ideas, then let them assume full responsibility for the kind of ideologies they choose to finance and support.[61]

Who are these new intellectuals?

> Any man or woman who is willing to think. All those who know that man's life must be guided by reason, those who value their own life and are not willing to surrender it to the cult of despair in the modern jungle of cynical impotence, just as they are not willing to surrender the world to the Dark Ages and the rule of the brutes.[62]

Unfortunately, there is an intellectual vacuum today. There is a real need for "the professional intellectual [who] is the field agent of the army whose commander-in-chief is the *philosopher*. The intellectual carries the application of philosophical principles to every

59. Rand, *New Intellectual*, p. 51.
60. Ibid.
61. Ibid., pp. 52 – 53.
62. Ibid., p. 50.

field of human endeavor."[63] It is the intellectuals who are true victors in the world. Rand asks, "Who is the conqueror of physical reality: the man who sleeps on a bed of nails or the man who sleeps on an inner-spring mattress? Which is the monument to the triumph of the human spirit over matter: the germ-eaten hovels of the shore-lines of the Ganges or the Atlantic skyline of New York?"[64] Obviously then, the primary social goal of the egocentric humanist is to fill the need for new intellectuals.

An Evaluation of Egocentric Humanism

Some Positive Features

There are a number of positive dimensions to Rand's view. Several may be briefly noted here.

First, her stress on reason as opposed to the irrationality of our day is commendable. Man is a rational being, and the right use of reason is necessary for the proper function of society.

Second, Rand's stress on the objective in ethics is good. A purely subjective ethic is not an ethic at all; it is chaos for society.

Third, there are many helpful insights in Rand's stress on the individual. In the final analysis every grouping of people, even society as a whole, is made up of individuals—individuals whose individual rights and liberties must be safeguarded.

Fourth, although Rand's brand of capitalism is extreme, her stress on economic freedom as an important dimension of a free society and her critiques of collectivism and communism are helpful.

Fifth, despite the radical form of self-love Rand embraces, there is a fundamental truth in her emphasis on human self-respect. Those who do not respect themselves probably will not respect others. Even Christianity teaches that one should love others as he loves himself (Matt. 22:39).

Some Negative Features

Despite the many appealing features of Rand's view we find some serious shortcomings when it is scrutinized carefully.

63. Ibid., p. 26.
64. Ibid., p. 171.

First, complete laissez-faire capitalism is unworkable, given the realities of human nature. As Thomas Hobbes said, man is a beast. It would take a world of angels to make Rand's system work. Even with good men, the smart will become richer, and the less fortunate will become poorer, unless limits are placed on the acquisition of wealth.

Second, Rand's egocentric humanism is really an intellectual elitism. The real dictators of the course of the world will be an elite core of intellectual egoists.

Third, there is really no ethical *duty* to anyone else—no obligation to help the less fortunate. Without such a duty selfish people will surely neglect the less fortunate.[65]

Fourth, there is really no ethical obligation or duty even to one's self. All "duties" turn out to be hypothetical; there are no categorical imperatives. Even the most basic values—such as reason, purpose, and self-esteem—are freely chosen *only if* one desires to survive. If one does not choose survival, then there are no such virtues.

Fifth, there are certain apparent inconsistencies in Rand's system. She denies God but speaks of His surrogate in phrases such as, "by the grace of reality [God?]."[66] She denies any ultimate Mind in the universe but speaks of the laws of thought as intrinsic laws which man discovers but did not create.[67] She denies ultimate obligations but speaks of "total dedication."[68]

Sixth, Rand commits the famous "is-ought" fallacy, for she insists that "to a living consciousness, every 'is' implies an 'ought.' "[69] If what *is* were what *ought* to be, then the status quo would always be one's moral duty.

Seventh, although Rand bemoans the fact that others have only replaced deity with society, she has substituted the individual for God: "Fight for the essence of that which is man: for his sovereign rational mind."[70]

Finally, if each human were an egocentric humanist, there would be no truly moral duty to any other human. And without at least some duty to humanity, how can one properly be called a humanist?

65. See Rand, *New Intellectual*, p. 180.
66. Rand, *Virtue*, p. 23.
67. Ibid., pp. 21 – 22.
68. Rand, *New Intellectual*, p. 192.
69. Rand, *Virtue*, p. 22.
70. Rand, *New Intellectual*, p. 192.

A FULLER TREATMENT &
EXCELLENT CRITIQUE IS FOUND
IN "CHRISTIANITY FOR THE
TOUGH MINDED" (EDITED BY J.W. MONTGOMERY)

7

Cultural Humanism

Of the many forms of humanism, one of the most influential in America is cultural humanism. For humanism's impact on our society has been largely a cultural one. In view of this it will be helpful to examine the basic ideas of one of the foremost proponents of the movement, Corliss Lamont. Lamont is a product of Ivy League education, being a graduate of Harvard and Cornell; he has also taught at both schools as well as Columbia. His views are articulated in his *The Philosophy of Humanism.*

The Basic Principles of Cultural Humanism

Lamont outlines ten basic principles of humanism. Their "task is to organize into a consistent and intelligible whole the chief elements of philosophic truth and to make that synthesis a powerful force and reality in the minds and actions of living men."[1]

Humanism has meant many things. It meant a reasonable balance of life to the Greeks. To some it is the study of the humanities. For others it is freedom from religiosity. Some think of humanism as a sensitivity to all humans. But Lamont believes that the greatest significance of humanism is as "a philosophy of which man is the center and sanction."

1. All the quotations under the heading "Basic Principles of Cultural Humanism" come from Corliss Lamont, *The Philosophy of Humanism* (New York: Philosophical Library, 1949), pp. 11 – 14.

Naturalism

The first principle of Lamont's humanism is naturalism. He writes, "Humanism believes in a naturalistic metaphysics or attitude toward the universe that considers all forms of the supernatural as myth." Humanism "regards Nature as the totality of being and as the constantly changing system of matter and energy which exists independently of any mind or consciousness."

Evolution and Materialism

"Second, Humanism, drawing especially upon the laws and facts of science, believes that man is an evolutionary product of Nature." This means that man's "mind is indivisibly cojoined with the functioning of his brain; and that as an inseparable unity of body and personality he can have no conscious survival after death." Thus evolutionism, materialism, and a denial of immortality are all interrelated.

Ultimate Faith in Man

The third principle of cultural humanism is that "Humanism, having its ultimate faith in man, believes that human beings possess the power or potentiality of solving their own problems." This can be accomplished "through reliance primarily upon reason and scientific method applied with courage and vision." In short, man can save himself and science is his means of doing it.

Genuine Human Freedom

"Fourth, Humanism [is] in opposition to all theories of universal determinism, fatalism, or predestination." Thus men, "while conditioned by the past, possess genuine freedom of creative choice and action and are, within certain objective limits, the masters of their own destiny." So man is truly free and capable of using that freedom to attain his own desired goals in life.

The Grounding of All Values in Earthly Experience

"Humanism believes in an ethics or morality that grounds all human values in this-earthly experiences." It also "holds as its highest goal the this-worldly happiness, freedom, and progress—economic, cultural, and ethical—of all mankind, irrespective of nation, race, or religion." This means situationism, not absolutism, in ethics.

Self-development by Doing Social Good

"Sixth, Humanism believes that the individual attains the good life by harmoniously combining personal satisfaction and continuous self-development with significant work ... that contributes to the welfare of the community." In brief, personal happiness comes from working for the social welfare of others.

Aesthetic Appreciation

"Humanism believes in the widest possible development of art and the awareness of beauty ... so that the aesthetic experience may become a pervasive reality in the life of men." This includes not only creative arts but also "the appreciation of Nature's loveliness and splendor." This emphasis on art and beauty is one of the hallmarks of cultural humanism.

Social Progress

"Eighth, Humanism believes in a far-reaching social program that stands for the establishment throughout the world of democracy, peace, and a high standard of living." This is to be built "on the foundation of a flourishing economic order, both national and international." Here the millennial aspirations of cultural humanism are evident.

Social Implementation of Science

How is the humanistic utopia to be attained? According to Lamont, it will be achieved by "the complete social implementation of reason and scientific method." This will include "full freedom of expression and civil liberties, throughout all areas of economic, political, and cultural life." In short, science used with full freedom by and for society can achieve personal and social happiness for mankind.

Unending Questioning of Basic Assumptions

"Tenth, Humanism ... believes in the unending questioning of basic assumptions and convictions, including its own." Humanism is not a dogma, says Lamont, "but is a developing philosophy ever open to experimental testing, newly discovered facts, and more rigorous reasoning." Thus cultural humanism remains skeptical and antidogmatic in its basic methodology. No basic principles, even humanistic ones, will be sacrosanct.

With these ten guiding principles cultural humanists hope to build a new world which will include an all-pervading humanistic culture.

The Requisites for a Humanistic Society

Lamont describes the forthcoming humanistic society: "A Humanistic civilization is one in which the principles of the Humanistic philosophy are dominant and find practical embodiment in laws, institutions, economics [and] culture."[2] He points out several items which are essential if such a society is to be achieved:

Democratization of Education and Culture

Lamont believes that "Humanism's thorough democratization of education and culture will result ... in a cultural flowering comparable in achievement to the outstanding epochs of the past and going far beyond them in breadth and impact." To achieve this "a Humanist society will invest in education and general cultural activity sums proportionate to what present-day governments allocate to armaments and war." With this financial support the potential of all types of students can be fully realized and humanistic goals achieved.

Promotion of Social Rather than Individual Goals

The full realization of the potential of each individual does not imply an individualism. For Lamont, "Humanist education naturally

2. All the quotations under the heading "Requisites for a Humanistic Society" come from *The Philosophy of Humanism*, pp. 273ff.

accents social rather than individualistic aims." This means more stress will be laid on social studies such as sociology, economics, politics, and ethics. Ethics is necessary "in order to train the youth of the nation in the broad Humanistic attitudes of loyalty to the social group and to humanity." This does not mean the physical sciences will be neglected. For "Humanism would also greatly extend the teaching of science and the scientific method." Lamont sees no necessary "opposition between science and the Humanities, from both of which the Humanist draws inspiration, and no concentration upon one of them to the exclusion of the other."

Spreading of Cultural Awareness

According to proponents of cultural humanism, the "educational program will be a large factor in spreading a fundamental awareness of literature and art among *all of the people*" (emphasis added). This means universal humanistic education is a necessity.

In order to achieve this unprecedented level of cultural attainment there must be complete freedom of expression. "The Humanist stress on complete cultural democracy and freedom of expression means that artists and writers should have the widest latitude in what they produce and say." That is, "a free art and a free literature are *absolute essentials* for a free culture" (emphasis added). For Lamont this freedom should exist for nonhumanist themes too: humanism "certainly will not bring pressure on art and literature to conform to any official philosophy; or seek to force the novel, the theatre, and the motion picture to deal with Humanist themes."

Removal of Moralistic Restraints on Artists and Writers

In order to attain this freedom of expression traditional moral restraints must be removed. "Narrow moralistic restraints on artists and writers have ever been a bane in the history of the west." These restraints, Lamont believes, "have frequently stemmed from the supernaturalists' suspicion of earthly pleasures." The quarrel has been that between the puritan and the artist. While the latter is "frankly interested in sensuous appearances," the former considers such a corruption of spirit. Lamont's position is that if cultural advancement is to be attained, all censorship must be eliminated.

Artistic Embodiment of Humanistic Themes

"One of the challenges to Humanist writers and artists will be to embody in artistic and literary works the general point of view for which Humanism stands." Lamont longs for a humanistic Michelangelo. For "genius is not confined to the delineation of any one philosophic position concerning the universe and man." Lamont senses that there is a great need for creative accomplishments representing the humanistic and naturalistic view.

The past has produced great poets representing various world views. Homer is the poet of paganism, Lucretius of materialism, Dante of Catholicism, Milton of Protestantism, Goethe of romanticism, and Wordsworth of pantheism. "As yet," laments Lamont, "no poet equal in rank to these just mentioned has put into enduring verse the basic themes of Humanism as a philosophy." The appearance of such a poet would be highly desirable for the humanist movement.

For the humanist art has a social origin and function. Art is not for God's sake; art is for man's sake. It is of the people, by the people, and for the people.

Humanistic Ceremony and Ritual

Another "essential function for artists and writers in a Humanist society will be to work out rituals and ceremonies consistent with central tenets of Humanism," writes Lamont. Such ceremonies should appeal to emotions as well as intellect, and thus provide people with an outlet for their delight in pomp and pageantry. For example, Christmas could be viewed "as a folk day symbolizing the joy of existence, the feeling of human brotherhood, and the ideal of democratic sharing." Further, "Easter can be humanistically utilized to celebrate the rebirth of the vital forces of Nature and the renewal of man's own energies." Also, humanists should make much of the birthdays of outstanding leaders of mankind and important anniversaries.

There is also the need for "wedding and funeral services based on a non-supernatural philosophy of life." Humanists not familiar with such services already in use (such as those prepared by Ethical Culture and Humanist groups) "tend to fall back on the traditional supernaturalist ceremonies." Lamont complains that this has unfortunately resulted in the false belief that humanists are really supernaturalists after all.

Priority of Human Rights

Humanists agree with Abraham Lincoln that "wherever there is a conflict between human rights and property rights, human rights must prevail." Thomas Jefferson was expressing much the same sentiment when he borrowed John Locke's statement of basic rights but changed the wording from "life, liberty and *property*" to "life, liberty and *the pursuit of happiness*." In this sense, then, the deistic framers of the Declaration of Independence were forefathers of contemporary cultural humanism.

Comprehensive Social Planning

Cultural humanism senses that it will not attain its goals without comprehensive social planning. "The first level of planning is ... problem-solving thought. The second level is a person's general planning for himself and his future." Then "the third level of planning is that which a family does for the well-being of its members." Beyond this is business planning, "national planning for the benefit of all the people through the means of coordinating the entire industrial and agricultural life of a country with transportation, finance, and distribution." Lamont does not see this as incompatible with democratic freedom.

Finally, "world planning for the welfare of all mankind is the highest and broadest level of all." This will involve a successful United Nations and "could lay the foundation for an integrated world economy and political federation."

Collective Security

No social scheme will be successful, Lamont contends, without the elimination of international war. Lamont believes that if one ignores the theistic implications, Immanuel Kant's *Perpetual Peace* (1795) is one of the best schemes for universal peace. It prescribes self-determination for all countries, general disarmament, and "a federation of free states agreeing to abolish war forever." This would result in a "State of Nations" or world republic, embracing all peoples.

In order to assure peace there must be "collective security." This means that "the peace-loving countries of the earth should band together against any aggressor or potential aggressor and speedily put an end, by means of collective action and mutual assistance, to war or the threat of war." This is a vital principle in international affairs.

A Sense of Moral Obligation to All Humanity

Since all nations are economically, politically, and culturally inter-related and interdependent, it follows that "every people has a moral obligation to humanity as a whole." This is a duty "to make common cause with the other peoples of the earth in man's eternal quest for peace, plenty and freedom. This is one world and we are all fellow citizens of it." Hence "a truly Humanist civilization must be a world civilization." And it is a moral duty for every nation to promote the concept of one world. Thus "Humanism is not only a philosophy with a world ideal, but an ideal philosophy for the world."

Affirmation of Man as His Own Savior

This world ideal for man is man's ideal for the world. And as a human ideal it finds its means as well as its source in man. In such a philosophy man "stands out as a far more heroic figure than in any of the supernaturalist creeds, old or new. He has become truly Prometheus Unbound with almost infinite powers and potentialities." Of course "for his achievements, man, utilizing the resources and laws of Nature, yet without Divine aid, can take full credit." Thus "Humanism assigns to man nothing less than the task of being his own savior and redeemer."

An Evaluation of Cultural Humanism

Some Positive Goals

Cultural humanism is all-encompassing. It sees no true happiness for men in isolation from one another. And in view of this it offers a comprehensive plan for uniting a fragmented world into one universal community of mankind. It is in effect a kind of cultural communism. In its utopian dream it offers many noble and commendable ideals.[3]

3. See Lamont, "The Affirmative Ethics of Humanism," *The Humanist* 40, no. 2 (March-April, 1980): 4 – 7, 53 – 54.

Universal freedom

Of all the goals of humanism few are more often repeated than that of freedom for all men. This freedom is not only political but also economic and aesthetic. Surely, as the cultural humanist believes, there will be no true happiness for man unless he is free. And there will be no universal happiness unless *all* are free.

Universal peace

If man is to achieve universal freedom, war must be abolished. In this the cultural humanist seems absolutely right. Unless the human race beats its swords into plowshares, universal peace will never be achieved. But given the realities of human nature, it seems unlikely that this can ever be accomplished short of some universal control.[4]

Universal government

Without a world government, world peace and unity are unachievable. Thus cultural humanists are correct in focusing on the goal of universal government. It is obvious that just as order is necessary to a happy life, world order is necessary to a happy world.

Universal education

One of the highest priorities of cultural humanism is education. Indeed, education is salvation, for intelligent foresight and planning are the key to a satisfying future. The cultural humanist must be commended for his dedication to education. Indeed, we should ever keep in mind the warning of the prophet Hosea: "My people are destroyed for lack of knowledge" (4:6).

Universal moral commitment

The commitment called for by cultural humanists is nothing short of religious. Although they deny any divine duty, they do deem man's moral duty divine. The moral obligation of man is not merely local or provincial; it is universal. It is, as Lamont says, "a moral obligation to humanity as a whole." The cultural humanist even speaks of his duty as an "absolute essential."[5] Lamont also insists there is a

4. See Lamont, "Affirmative Ethics," p. 6.
5. Lamont, *The Philosophy of Humanism*, pp. 273ff.

"supreme ethical end"—the Community Good.[6] Such unconditional moral commitment is surely praiseworthy.

There are, of course, other fine features of cultural humanism, such as its concern for human conditions and its desire for aesthetic enrichment of life. The features we have just discussed, however, will suffice to indicate the cultural humanist's desire to contribute to the happiness of mankind.

Some Negative Features

Cultural humanism is not without its problems. Some of our criticism has to do with the fact that cultural humanism lacks the means to achieve its noble goals. Other criticisms focus on internal tensions in the system.

Inadequate means

One would not disagree with the humanist's noble goals; rather, the problem is that his means of attaining them is inadequate. Science and human reason alone have proven insufficient in controlling the human heart.[7] Even if science could control the external world, there is no evidence to demonstrate that it could control the internal world (that is, men's thoughts and wills) without destroying it. There is no evidence from thousands of years of human history to support the naive assumption of humanists that man can successfully control his own destiny. Lamont virtually admits humanism's inability to inspire men to greater achievements (at least in art) when he points out that no great humanist poet has arisen. In fact, no great humanist moralist has arisen either. Most of the great moral principles and goals of humanism are borrowed from philosophers who believed in God (for example, Locke, Jefferson, Kant, and John Stuart Mill).[8]

Internal inconsistencies

The first inconsistency on which we will focus is that while cultural humanism calls for a world government, it at the same time affirms democracy and self-determination for all people. But one

6. See Lamont, "Affirmative Ethics," p. 6.
7. See J. W. N. Sullivan, *The Limitations of Science* (1933; repr. ed., New York: New American Library, 1956).
8. See T. M. Kitwood, *What Is Human?* (Downers Grove, Ill.: Inter-Varsity, 1970).

cannot have it both ways. If one government controls all nations, then no one nation controls itself.

Second, cultural humanists call for freedom of expression for all points of view (even nonhumanist views), yet they insist on universal *humanist* education in values, art, and literature.[9] This is analogous to the very thing humanists detest in certain religions. For they allege that these religions, while claiming everyone is free to worship (or not worship) as he will, yet insist on an acknowledgment of their deity as part of public education. Apparently the humanists are guilty of the very inconsistencies they see in others. In theory they reject the imposition of any "official philosophy," but in practice they would make humanism the official philosophy of mankind.

Third, humanists claim that man evolved from matter, that he has no immortal soul, that he is a purely finite, temporal being. However, they believe man has infinite potential and is of absolute or ultimate value. But surely what is merely finite has no infinite worth and what is only immediate and mortal has no ultimate value.

Fourth, the humanists' call for complete freedom of expression permits even moral and religious themes in art, yet they reject the religious as a hindrance to cultural advancement and insist on a purely naturalistic view of the universe. This is tantamount to saying they will universally educate children to believe religion is primitive, regressive, and even antihuman. But if anyone is still dumb enough to want to draw a religious picture they will give him the crayons and paper (pigment and canvas will be reserved for humanists!).

Finally, Lamont does not seem to take seriously his own exhortation that every system engage in an "unending questioning of basic assumptions and convictions, including its own." For nowhere in his book does Lamont show the slightest inclination to question seriously his own basic naturalistic and humanistic presuppositions. On

9. See "A Secular Humanist Declaration," in *Free Inquiry*, Winter 1980 – 81, for a classic example of this. Page 4 reads, "The lessons of history are clear: wherever one religion or ideology is established and given a dominant position in the state, minority opinions are in jeopardy. A pluralistic, open-democratic society allows all points of view to be heard." Yet only two pages later we read, "We deplore the efforts by fundamentalists (especially in the United States) to invade the science classrooms, requiring that creationist theory be taught to students and requiring that it be included in biology textbooks. This is a serious threat both to academic freedom and to the integrity of the educational process."

the contrary, there is every evidence that a naturalistic hardening of the arteries has set in.

Cultural humanism has many broad and helpful goals for mankind, including freedom, peace, political security, education, and the realization of moral values. However, while these *goals* are good, the humanist does not have the *means* of attaining them. Man has not proven himself capable of attaining his own utopia. Furthermore, there are many tensions or conflicts within cultural humanism which appear to render the view incoherent. How can all nations be truly free and yet exist under one world government? How can humanists insist man is of ultimate value when man is not ultimate? For they admit that even the human race is mortal in the long run.

Christian Humanism

There are many kinds of humanism. Not all of them are atheistic. In fact some forms of humanism are not only theistic, they are Christian.

The Roots of Christian Humanism

Christian humanism is not new. It goes back to the earliest centuries of Christianity, when there were Christian humanists like Justin Martyr and Origen. In later antiquity and the Middle Ages there were Augustine and Thomas Aquinas. At the time of the Reformation Erasmus exemplified Christian humanism. And indeed, some of the Reformers, such as Martin Luther and John Calvin, placed emphasis on what we call the humanities, thus accenting human values.

Christian humanism has received some of its most articulate expression in the Anglo-Catholic tradition. John Henry Cardinal Newman's *Idea of a University* is a classic expression of this philosophy. The French neo-Thomist Jacques Maritain also articulated a Catholic humanism in his *True Humanism*.[1]

Perhaps the most popular and widely read expression of modern Christian humanism is that of the Oxford Christian group, which included C. S. Lewis, Charles Williams, and J. R. R. Tolkien.

The Nature of Christian Humanism

We will use the writings of C. S. Lewis as our primary example of Christian humanism. Lewis devotes a good bit of space in his writ-

---

1. Jacques Maritain, *True Humanism* (New York: Books for Libraries, 1970).

ings to attacking secular humanism. He speaks out against its naturalistic basis in *Miracles*. He attacks its insidious political potential in *That Hideous Strength*.[2] He writes against its pseudojustice in his article opposed to the reformatory view of justice (i.e., the view that those guilty of crime should be forced into programs aimed at reforming them).[3] But the essence of C. S. Lewis's view, which we have called Christian humanism, is best expounded in *The Abolition of Man*[4] and *Mere Christianity*.[5] First let us examine Lewis's critique of secular humanism. Then we will be better able to see the shape of his Christian humanism.

The Attack on Secular Humanism

There are many aspects of secular humanism which Lewis critiques. The most fundamental are its view of God, miracles, and morals.

Secular humanism's view of God

Lewis is well aware of the atheism implied (or stated) in secular humanism. To counteract this, the first part of *Mere Christianity* is devoted to a moral argument for the existence of God.

Lewis's argument can be summarized as follows. There must be an objective, universal moral law, or else none of our ethical judgments would make any sense. Such judgments as "The Nazis were wrong" would be meaningless, and there would be no reason to keep promises or treaties.[6] This moral law does not originate with us. In fact, we find ourselves bound by it. The source of this law is more like mind than matter, and it cannot be part of the universe any more than an architect is part of the building he designs. Therefore, there exists a moral Lawgiver who is the ultimate source and standard of all right and wrong.[7]

Secular humanism's view of morals

In the process of developing his moral argument for God, Lewis takes the opportunity to critique humanistic alternatives to an objec-

2. C. S. Lewis, *That Hideous Strength* (New York: Macmillan, 1946).

3. Lewis, "The Humanitarian Theory of Punishment," in *God in the Dock: Essays on Theology and Ethics*, ed. Walter Hooper (Grand Rapids: Eerdmans, 1970).

4. Lewis, *The Abolition of Man* (New York: Macmillan, 1947).

5. Lewis, *Mere Christianity* (New York: Macmillan, 1943).

6. Ibid., p. 25.

7. Ibid., p. 39.

tive moral law. The moral law cannot be instinct as some humanists suggest, says Lewis. If it were then the stronger impulse would always prevail. But sometimes the moral law sides with the weaker impulse. Even the instinct of self-preservation is sometimes at odds with one's duty to do right.[8]

Also, the contention of some secular humanists that moral law (since it is something we learn) is only a social convention is countered by Lewis. For not everything learned is strictly an arbitrary choice of society; the laws of mathematics are a good example. Furthermore, argues Lewis, moral judgment and moral progress make no sense if the bases of our judgments are strictly social conventions.[9]

Finally, one cannot, as some humanists do, regard morality for himself as nothing other than his own present situation. "Ought" does not reduce to "is." Nor can morality be reduced to what is convenient. What may be convenient (e.g., being a traitor under pressure) is not necessarily right, and what may be inconvenient (e.g., accidentally tripping someone) is not necessarily morally wrong.[10]

Secular humanism's view of miracles

Another premise of secular humanism Lewis concentrates on is naturalism. The heart of his critique is found in "The Self-Contradiction of the Naturalist," a chapter in his book *Miracles*. Lewis's argument against naturalism can be summarized in the following manner: Naturalism claims that nature is the "whole show." So if naturalism is true, then every event in nature must be explicable in terms of the total system of nature. But human (inferential) reason, such as even naturalists assume and exercise, cannot be explained strictly in terms of nonrational natural causes. Moreover, "the Naturalist cannot condemn other people's thoughts because they have irrational causes and continue to believe his own which have (if Naturalism is true) equally irrational causes."[11] Furthermore, argues Lewis, if naturalism is right then there is no reason that the thoughts of a lunatic or drug addict should not be valued by a naturalist as much as his own thoughts. This, Lewis insists, is the "self-contradiction" of naturalism.[12]

8. Ibid., pp. 22 – 23.
9. Ibid., pp. 24 – 25.
10. Ibid., p. 28.
11. Lewis, *Miracles* (New York: Macmillan, 1947), p. 22.
12. In a subsequent (British) edition Lewis modified this description from "self-contradiction" to "cardinal difficulty," but he never gave up his central point.

Secular humanism's view of education

The first part of *The Abolition of Man* is devoted to a critique of a humanistic theory of education. Lewis asserts that through such means as elementary texts on grammar, schools attempt to change values without the pupil's being aware of it. This, says Lewis, is like returning from a dentist with your teeth untouched but your head crammed with philosophy.[13] Especially objectionable to Lewis is the implication of some secular humanists that our value judgments "appear to be saying something very important about something: and actually we are only saying something about our own feelings."[14] This is "not a theory they put into [a person's] mind, but an assumption, which ten years hence, its origin forgotten and its presence unconscious, will condition him to take one side in a controversy which he has never recognized as a controversy at all."[15]

Such subtly taught assumptions result in changed attitudes toward values. This, Lewis holds, is bad education. For "the task of the modern educator is not to cut down jungles but to irrigate deserts." Instead, the educator "may be intending to make a clean sweep of traditional values and start with a new set."[16] This will not be fruitful, says Lewis. For "the right defense against false sentiment is to inculcate just sentiment." And further, "famished nature will be avenged and a hard heart is no infallible protection against a soft head."[17] Thus an education where feeling dominates thinking is a foolish form of humanism. Values are not purely subjective. There is an objective basis for our feelings and value judgments, a basis which education must cultivate, not contradict.

Secular humanism's view of justice

So biased against Lewis's penal view of justice were the British secular humanists of his day that they would not publish an article he wrote on the topic. It was first published in an Australian journal (and later incorporated into *God in the Dock*). In this article Lewis attacks secular humanism's reformatory view of justice. He argues that it is tyrannical to submit a man to a compulsory cure unless he

13. Lewis, *The Abolition of Man*, p. 23.
14. Ibid., p. 14.
15. Ibid., pp. 16 – 17.
16. Ibid., p. 23.
17. Ibid., p. 24.

desires it. Lewis calls the reformatory view an "illusory humanitarianism" which disguises possible cruelty and injustice. It is built on the false premise that crime is pathological, not moral. In fact, the reformatory view dehumanizes the individual, treating him as a patient or case rather than as a person. Lewis insisted that "to be 'cured' against one's will . . . is to be put on a level with those who have not yet reached the age of reason or those who never will; to be classed with infants, imbeciles, and domestic animals." On the other hand, "to be punished, however severely, because we have deserved it, because we 'ought to have known better,' is to be treated as a human person made in God's image."[18]

Secular humanism's hideous political potential

Lewis was keenly aware of the danger of replacing the objective moral law of God with the subjective political laws of man. History shows that dictators who step outside the moral law are invariably not benevolent. And the potential for evil when great power resides in man's political grasp is horrendous. This point Lewis makes masterfully in his book *That Hideous Strength*.

Secular humanism's attempt to control nature through science

Lewis speaks of another aspect of secular humanism—the attempt to control nature. He believes both magic and science have the same motivation—the desire to control the world.[19] Lewis chides the humanists for their boast that "Man has Nature whacked."[20] For "as regards the powers manifested in the aeroplane or the wireless, man is as much the patient or subject as the possessor, since he is the target both for bombs and for propaganda."[21] In point of fact, "what we call Man's power over Nature turns out to be a power exercised by some men over other men with Nature as its instrument."[22]

Furthermore, says Lewis, as the human species approaches its ultimate extinction (according to the humanists), the less power over the race man has. So as the power of man increases, the longevity

18. Lewis, "The Humanitarian Theory of Punishment," p. 292.
19. Lewis, *The Abolition of Man*, p. 87.
20. Ibid., p. 67.
21. Ibid., p. 68.
22. Ibid., p. 69.

of the race diminishes. Consequently "the last men, far from being the heirs of power ... will themselves exercise least power upon the future." Thus "each new power won *by* man is a power *over* man as well. Each advance leaves him weaker as well as stronger."[23]

Even if man gains the final eugenic power to make himself what he pleases, this is really only "the power of some men to make other men what they please."[24] Unless men are bound by an objective moral law, the power gained will be used only to bind man, not to benefit him. For, says Lewis, "I am very doubtful whether history shows us one example of a man who, having stepped outside traditional morality and attained power, has used that power benevolently."[25] And the final irony is that when men step outside the moral law (which Lewis calls the *Tao*, the Chinese word for "way"), "they are not men at all: they are artifacts. Man's final conquest has proved to be the abolition of Man."[26]

The Structure of Christian Humanism

From the rubble of Lewis's critique of secular humanism we can see what shape his own Christian humanism would take. We discover that Lewis does not deny man nor his powers but affirms them.

Affirming man's rationality

Lewis would not blush at the appellation "rationalist." Repeatedly he exalts human rational powers. He writes, "I couldn't get at the universe unless I could trust my reason. If we couldn't trust inference we could know nothing but our own existence."[27] "The heart never takes the place of the head; but can and should obey it."[28]

Lewis insists that there must be an ultimate Reason or Explanation. For "you cannot go on 'explaining away' forever: you will find that you have explained explanation itself away." Moreover, "you cannot go on 'seeing through things forever.' " Consequently "it is no use trying to 'see through' first principles. If you see through everything,

23. Ibid., p. 71.
24. Ibid., p. 72.
25. Ibid., p. 75.
26. Ibid., p. 77.
27. Lewis, "Bulverism," in *God in the Dock*, p. 277.
28. Lewis, *The Abolition of Man*, p. 30.

then everything is transparent." But "to 'see through' all things is the same as not to see."[29]

Lewis believes rational thought is undeniable. He insists that "all arguments [against] the validity of thought make a tacit, and illegitimate, exception in favor of the bit of thought you are doing at that moment." Hence "the validity of thought is central: all other things have to be fitted in round it as best they can."[30]

Affirming man's morality

Placing emphasis on man's rational nature does not negate his emotions. "The head rules the belly through the chest—the seat ... of emotions organized by trained habit into stable sentiments." In fact, "it may even be said that [without] this middle element ... man is vain: for by his intellect he is mere spirit and by his appetite mere animal."[31] Thus it is an outrage that those secular humanists who affirm man's rational nature without recognizing his moral nature should be called intellectuals. For "their heads are no bigger than the ordinary: it is the atrophy of the chest beneath that makes them seem so."[32]

Not only does man have a moral nature, but there is also a moral ideal which he can work to attain. In fact, it is the proper purpose of education to cultivate man's value judgments and help perfect his moral nature. For "without the aid of trained emotions the intellect is powerless against the animal organism."[33] Thus, Lewis observes, it is better to play cards with a skeptic who is a gentleman than with a moral philosopher who was brought up among card sharks.[34] Because man stands within God's law "we can speak of Man having power over himself in a sense truly analogous to an individual's self-control."[35] Thus we must educate men in virtue.

Secular humanism in contrast to Christian humanism in a sort of ghastly simplicity removes the moral organ and yet demands the moral function. "We make men without chests and expect of them virtue and enterprise. We laugh at honour and are shocked to find

29. Ibid., p. 91.
30. Lewis, *Miracles*, p. 23.
31. Lewis, *The Abolition of Man*, p. 34.
32. Ibid., p. 35.
33. Ibid., pp. 33 – 34.
34. Ibid., p. 34.
35. Ibid., p. 86.

traitors in our midst."[36] Although these words are not Lewis's own, he would agree that the primary value of an education is an education in primary values.

Affirming man's creative ability

A characteristic feature of the Christian humanism of C. S. Lewis is the affirmation of man's aesthetic nature. Lewis not only affirmed man's aesthetic ability, he exemplified it. He and the other Oxford Christians produced an immense literary output. Lewis wrote the seven books of the Narnia series and the space trilogy along with his famous *Screwtape Letters* and numerous other Christian writings from *Mere Christianity* to *Reflections on the Psalms.*[37] On top of this he wrote numerous articles as well as *Studies in Medieval and Renaissance Literature.*[38] J. R. R. Tolkien has also produced some high-quality and very popular literature such as *The Lord of the Rings.*[39]

The basic philosophy of aesthetics behind these Oxford Christian humanists is articulated in Dorothy Sayers's "Toward a Christian Esthetic": "This word—this idea of art as *creation*—is, I believe, the one important contribution that Christianity has made to esthetics."[40] Man is not the Creator, but he is a subcreator. And by exercising this creative ability man expresses in images his inner feelings even as the Invisible God was visibly expressed in the incarnation of His Son.

Affirming man's immortality

What characterizes Christian humanism perhaps more than anything else is its affirmation of man's eternal value. This affirmation springs from the belief that man is made in God's image. To affirm man while denying his ultimate moral value does not affirm man's real value at all. Secular humanists, Lewis believes, do not affirm man; rather, they abolish man. For in denying man's immortal, moral,

36. Ibid., p. 35.

37. Lewis, *Screwtape Letters* (New York: Collins, 1979), and *Reflections on the Psalms* (New York: Collins, 1958).

38. Lewis, *Studies in Medieval and Renaissance Literature* (New York: Cambridge, 1966).

39. J. R. R. Tolkien, *The Lord of the Rings* (Boston: Houghton Mifflin, 1979).

40. Dorothy Sayers, "Toward a Christian Esthetic," in *The Whimsical Christian* (New York: Macmillan, 1978), p. 83.

and Godlike nature they deny his manness and sweep away the basis for treating man with ultimate respect.[41]

The irony, then, is this. Secular humanists would make man ultimate, but in so doing they sweep away man's right to be treated with ultimate respect. By contrast Christian humanism, in affirming that the basis for man's ultimate value comes not from man but from God, has preserved the basis for showing ultimate respect to man.

Secular humanism dehumanizes man. Only Christian humanism retains man's true humanness. Lewis holds that "either we are rational spirit obliged for ever to obey the absolute values of the *Tao*, or else we are mere nature to be kneaded and cut into new shapes."[42] Thus the only guarantee against tryanny and slavery is to affirm man's immortal value in the context of an absolute moral law. For "the process which, if not checked, will abolish Man, goes on apace among Communists and Democrats no less than among Fascists."[43] Only within the absolute moral law do "we find the concrete reality in which to participate is to be truly human."[44]

Affirming man's dignity

Following from man's rationality and moral responsibility is his human dignity. There is a firm basis for this virtue in man's immortal, Godlike nature: man has rational, moral, and volitional abilities. This is why a man is punished when he does wrong—because he knew better and deserves to be penalized for his action.[45] Punishment is a compliment to man's dignity.

Lewis also offers an exhortation to modern science in view of man's dignity. Citing Martin Buber, Lewis warns science not to treat man as an "It" but to recognize him as a "Thou."[46] We must never surrender man to science as a mere object to be controlled. This, says Lewis, is "a 'magician's bargain' ... whereby man surrenders object after object, and finally himself, to Nature in return for power."[47] Lewis contends that when science is allowed to take control, it has the same goal as magic, though its means differ.[48] He reminds us

41. Lewis, *The Abolition of Man*, pp. 76 — 77.
42. Ibid., p. 84.
43. Ibid., p. 85.
44. Ibid., p. 86.
45. See quote on p. 99 (n. 18).
46. Lewis, *The Abolition of Man*, p. 90.
47. Ibid., p. 87.
48. Ibid., p. 89.

that even the father of modern science, Francis Bacon, condemns those who make scientific knowledge an end in itself, rather than a means of control.[49] Lewis calls science to "repentance" and adds, "The regenerate science which I have in mind would not do even to minerals and vegetables what modern science threatens to do to man himself."[50] For science's "triumphs may have been too rapid and purchased at too high a price: reconsideration, and something like repentance may be required."[51]

An Evaluation of Christian Humanism

Since the many positive features of Christian humanism have already been stressed in this chapter we will concentrate here on some of its weaknesses and dangers.

The Need for a Clear Definition

To many the words *Christian* and *humanistic* are contradictions in terms. Indeed, by some definitions they are. So it behooves us to specify what is meant by *humanism*. In brief, humanism is a philosophy which affirms the value of what is human, or which holds that humans have value in and of themselves. For at the center of all forms of humanism—secular, Christian, or whatever—there is an emphasis on the worth of man. There is the belief that man has value worth pursuing. Man is in some sense the center and focus of activity. His abilities are to be exercised and he is to be highly regarded. Thus the humanities and the arts are to be studied and science is to be developed. Man has intrinsic value; therefore what he thinks, creates, and performs also has great value. In this sense of the term *humanism* there is Christian humanism. And C. S. Lewis's writings are certainly a prime example of it.

The Need for a Clear Distinction

Even in the light of our definition of humanism, a clearer distinction still must be made. While there is a core of beliefs common to

49. Ibid., p. 88.
50. Ibid., pp. 89 – 90.
51. Ibid., p. 89.

all forms of humanism, there is also a stark contrast between Christian and secular humanism. Whereas both hold that man is an end, for the Christian humanity is not an *ultimate* end. While man is the *center* of activity in the world, he is not the final *goal* of history. Furthermore, man is only the *focus* of life, not the *basis* of it. Man is the maker of many things on earth, but he is not the Maker of heaven and earth. In short, man is able to measure many things, but man is not the measure of all things. For man is himself made and measured by God. These are crucial differences between Christian and secular humanism.

Some Problems with C. S. Lewis's Christian Humanism

It is never popular to critique a "saint" or a spiritual hero. Nonetheless, it is sometimes necessary. Certainly Lewis admirably upheld the humanistic aspect of his Christian humanism. And he held a rather historic Anglo-Catholic orthodoxy with respect to the "Christian" aspect. However, at times he fell into the secular humanistic approach he critiqued.

Lewis's naturalistic views

Lewis wrote one of the finest critiques of naturalism in print (*Miracles*). In this book he defended the literal nature of New Testament miracles, including the resurrection of Christ. Nevertheless, while he was defending New Testament miracles, at the same time Lewis denied many Old Testament miracles:

> The Hebrews, like other peoples, had mythology: but as they were the chosen people so their mythology was the chosen mythology—the mythology chosen by God to be the vehicle of the earliest sacred truths, the first step in that process which ends in the New Testament where truth has become completely historical. Whether we can ever say with certainty where, in this process of crystalisation, any particular Old Testament story falls, is another matter. I take it that the memoirs of David's court come at one end of the scale and are scarcely less historical than *St. Mark* or *Acts*; and that the *Book of Jonah* is at the opposite end.[52]

Lewis accepts the deity of Christ. But it was Christ who verified the historicity and authenticity of some of the very Old Testament

52. Lewis, *Miracles*, p. 139, n. 1.

events Lewis rejects. Jesus verified the literal truth of Jonah (Matt. 12:40), of the creation of Adam and Eve (Matt. 19:4), of Noah and the flood (Matt. 24:38 – 39), and of many other miraculous Old Testament events.[53] Here Lewis seems to be reading into the Old Testament his own (humanistically derived?) view of the development of a myth. This is especially surprising in view of his penetrating criticism of New Testament scholars who do the same thing. Lewis chides them:

> A theology which denies the historicity of nearly everything in the Gospels to which Christian life and affections and thought have been fastened for nearly two millennia—which either denies the miraculous altogether or, more strangely, after swallowing the camel of the Resurrection strains at such gnats as the feeding of the multitudes—if offered to the uneducated man can produce only one or other of two effects.[54]

The mitigating factor in Lewis's inconsistency is his own recognition that his view on Old Testament miracles might be wrong. For he admits that this view is tentative and liable to error, and that the subject matter is beyond his scope of knowledge:

> A consideration of the Old Testament miracles is beyond the scope of this book and would require many kinds of knowledge which I do not possess. My present view—which is tentative and liable to any amount of correction—would be that just as, on the factual side, a long preparation culminates in God's becoming incarnate as Man, so, on the documentary side, the truth first appears in *mythical* form and then by a long process of condensing or focussing finally becomes incarnate as History.[55]

Lewis's higher criticism of the Bible

Not only did Lewis's naturalistic interpretation of Old Testament miracles reveal a secular humanistic influence, but he also accepted much of the negative criticism of other Old Testament events or writings. He questioned the historicity of Job: "The *Book of Job* appears to me unhistorical because it begins about a man quite unconnected

53. See John Wenham, "Christ's View of Scripture," in *Inerrancy,* ed. N. L. Geisler (Grand Rapids: Zondervan), 1980, pp. 3 – 35.
54. Lewis, "Modern Theology and Biblical Criticism," in *Christian Reflections* (Grand Rapids: Eerdmans, 1967), p. 139.
55. Lewis, *Miracles,* p. 139, n. 1.

with all history or even legend, with no genealogy, living in a country of which the Bible elsewhere has hardly anything to say."[56] Lewis held this in spite of the fact that both the Old (Ezek. 14:14, 20) and the New Testaments (James 5:11) refer to Job as historical, and there is mention elsewhere of the land in which he lived (Jer. 25:20; Lam. 4:21). In addition the authenticity of many customs and proper names in the books has been verified.[57]

Lewis held a very negative view of many of the Psalms, even calling some "devilish,"[58] and rejecting the Davidic authorship of all but one Psalm (18).[59] This latter view is especially surprising when one considers Lewis's high view of Christ and the Gospels. For Jesus personally verified that David wrote Psalm 110 (cf. Matt. 22). Jesus also affirmed the divine authority of the whole Old Testament (Matt. 5:17 – 18; John 10:35) and especially the Psalms (cf. Luke 24:44), which was one of the books He quoted most.

These are not the only ways in which Lewis came under the negative influence of secular thought,[60] but they illustrate that the Christian humanist must maintain a constant vigil to make sure he has a *Christian* view of what is human and not a *humanistic* view of what is Christian.

56. Lewis, *Reflections on the Psalms*, p. 110.

57. See Gleason Archer, *A Survey of Old Testament Introduction* (Chicago: Moody, 1964), pp. 438 – 448.

58. Lewis, *Reflections on the Psalms*, p. 25.

59. Lewis wrote, "How old the Psalms, as we now have them, really are is a question for the scholars. I am told there is one (No. 18) which might really have come down from the age of David himself; that is, from the tenth century B.C. Most of them, however, are said to be 'post exilic'; the book was put together when the Hebrews, long exiled in Babylonia, were repatriated by that enlightened ruler, Cyrus of Persia" (*Reflections on the Psalms*, p. 114).

60. Lewis also held an evolutionary, rather than a creationistic, view of the universe's origin (see *Mere Christianity*, pp. 52, 65).

An Evaluation of Contemporary Humanism

9

Secular Humanism

In Part One we examined a variety of kinds of humanism. Each kind, as we have seen, has its own distinctive emphases. There is, however, a central core of beliefs that the non-Christian (or non-theistic) forms of humanism share. The name most often given to the philosophy which embraces these beliefs is secular humanism. In Part Two we will examine and evaluate both the strong and weak points of this movement. We begin in this chapter by presenting the central beliefs of this philosophy as they have been articulated in some of its "creeds."

"Humanist Manifesto I"

Secular humanists have sometimes formed coalitions to produce declarations of their beliefs. In 1933 a group of thirty-four American humanists enunciated the fundamental principles of their philosophy in "Humanist Manifesto I." The signatories included John Dewey, father of American pragmatic education; Edwin A. Burtt, a philosopher of religion; and R. Lester Mondale, a Unitarian minister (and brother of Walter Mondale, former vice-president of the United States).

In the preamble to this manifesto the authors identify themselves as "religious humanists," and affirm that "to establish such a religion is a major necessity of the present."[1] The manifesto consists of fifteen basic affirmations:

1. "Humanist Manifesto I," in *Humanist Manifestos I & II*, ed. Paul Kurtz (Buffalo: Prometheus, 1973).

"*First*: Religious humanists regard the universe as self-existing and not created." They are nontheists, denying that there is a Creator. The universe is self-sufficient, needing no God to bring it into existence nor to sustain it.

"*Second*: Humanism believes that man is a part of nature and that he has emerged as the result of a continuous process." Two beliefs are implied here: naturalism and evolutionism. If there is no Creator, then of course there is no such thing as the supernatural. And likewise if there is no Creator, then life was not created but evolved.

"*Third*: Holding an organic view of life, humanists find that the traditional dualism of mind and body must be rejected." This affirmation entails two beliefs. First, man has no "soul" or immaterial aspect to his nature. Second, man is not immortal; he will not survive death and live forever.

"*Fourth*: Humanism recognizes that man's religious culture and civilization ... are the product of a gradual development." Further, "the individual born into a particular culture is largely molded to that culture." This implies cultural evolution and cultural relativity. Cultural evolution means that human society has gradually become more sophisticated and complex; cultural relativity means that individuals are shaped largely by their particular cultures.

"*Fifth*: Humanism asserts that the nature of the universe depicted by modern science makes unacceptable any supernatural or cosmic guarantee of human values." Here humanists affirm that all values are manmade and not divine. There are no God-given values for humans to discover; man determines his own values. Therefore values are relative and subject to change.

"*Sixth*: We are convinced that the time has passed for theism, deism, modernism, and several varieties of 'new thought.'" The framers of the first manifesto claim to be atheists in the traditional sense of the word. Even the desupernaturalized form of belief in God called "deism" is rejected.

"*Seventh*: Religion consists of those actions, purposes, and experiences which are humanly significant ... all that is in its degree expressive of intelligently satisfying human living." The essence of this affirmation is to define religion in purely humanistic terms, thus excluding God. Religion then consists of anything that is significant or interesting or satisfying to humans.

"*Eighth*: Religious humanism considers the complete realization of human personality to be the end of man's life and seeks its development and fulfillment in the here and now." The hope of the humanist is this-worldly. The chief end of man is terrestrial, not celestial.

"*Ninth*: In place of the old attitudes involved in worship and prayer the humanist finds his religious emotions expressed in a heightened sense of personal life and in a cooperative effort to promote social well-being." The religious emotion is focused in the natural, personal, and social spheres, not in the spiritual or the supernatural realms.

"*Tenth*: It follows that there will be no uniquely religious emotions and attitudes of the kind hitherto associated with belief in the supernatural." This point carries out the naturalistic implications of earlier statements: even religious experience must be explained in purely nonsupernatural terms.

"*Eleventh*: Man will learn to face the crises of life in terms of his knowledge of their naturalness and probability." Humanists believe that humanistic education will promote social well-being by discouraging the wishful thinking and worrying that stem from ignorance.

"*Twelfth*: Believing that religion must work increasingly for joy in living, religious humanists aim to foster the creative in man and to encourage achievements that add to satisfactions in life." In stressing the humanistic values of creativity and achievement, this point shows the influence of John Dewey.

"*Thirteenth*: Religious humanism maintains that all associations and institutions exist for the fulfillment of human life." In view of this, humanists insist that religious institutions, their ritualistic forms, ecclesiastical methods, and communal activities must be reconstituted as rapidly as possible, in order to function effectively in the modern world. Here is a zealous iconoclasm aimed at traditional religion.

"*Fourteenth*: The humanists are firmly convinced that existing acquisitive and profit-motivated society has shown itself to be inadequate and that radical change in methods, controls, and motives must be instituted." In lieu of capitalism humanists suggest "a socialized and cooperative economic order." "Humanist Manifesto I," then, reflects an anticapitalist and prosocialist tendency.

"*Fifteenth and last*: We assert that humanism will: (a) affirm life rather than deny it; (b) seek to elicit the possibilities of life, not flee from it; and (c) endeavor to establish the conditions of a satisfactory life for all, not merely for the few." Besides the obvious attempt to put religious humanism in a positive (i.e., life-affirming) framework, there is an implied socialism here too.

In conclusion, the religious humanists who framed the manifesto affirmed that "the quest for the good life is still the central task for mankind" and that man "has within himself the power for its achievement." Thus they were optimistic with respect to their goals and perfectionistic in their belief that man has the ability to achieve them.

"Humanist Manifesto I" can be summarized as (1) atheistic regarding the existence of God, (2) naturalistic regarding the possibility of miracles, (3) evolutionistic concerning man's origin, (4) relativistic concerning values, (5) optimistic about the future, (6) socialistic in political view, (7) religious in attitude toward life, and (8) humanistic with regard to the methods which it suggests to those who would achieve its goals.

Several observations should be made in reviewing this statement. First, it is obviously overly optimistic. Even the framers of "Humanist Manifesto II" (1973) acknowledged that "events since [1933] make that earlier statement seem far too optimistic."

Second, "Humanist Manifesto I" studiously avoids use of the words *ought* and *should*. It does not, however, avoid equivalent terms such as *will* (art. 15) and *must* (arts. 3, 5, 12, 13, 14). In addition, the humanists' affirmation of certain values (that which they consider worthwhile) implies that one "ought" to pursue those values. Hence the secular humanists are in effect offering moral prescriptions which they believe humans ought to follow.

Third, some of the moral prescriptions implied have a universal force. This is evidenced by the repeated use of words like *necessity* (preamble), *must* (arts. 3, 5, 12), *insists* (art. 5), *no* (or *nothing*—arts. 7, 10, conclusion), and even *demand* (art. 14) in connection with the values being advocated. In the preamble a universal obligation is euphemistically called an "abiding value." Likewise, the values of freedom, creativity, and achievement are clearly regarded as universal and irrevocable.

Fourth, it is worth noting that the religious tone of the first manifesto is very evident: the word *religion* (or *religious*) occurs in it some twenty-eight times. The authors consider themselves religious, wish to preserve religious experience, and even call themselves religious humanists. Their religion, however, is without an ultimate personal object of religious experience (God).

"Humanist Manifesto II"

In 1973, forty years after the framing of "Humanist Manifesto I,"
proponents of secular humanism from several countries felt an
updating was necessary and consequently formulated "Humanist
Manifesto II."[2] This document was signed by such notables as the
author Isaac Asimov; professors Brand Blanshard, Antony Flew, and
A. J. Ayer; psychologist B. F. Skinner; situational ethicist Joseph Fletcher;
and biologist Jacques Monod.

In the preface to their manifesto the authors deny that they "are
setting forth a binding credo," but say that "for today it is our conviction." They do acknowledge their continuity with earlier humanists in affirming that God, prayer, salvation, and providence are part
of "an unproved and outmoded faith."

There are seventeen basic affirmations in "Humanist Manifesto II."
They appear under the headings "religion" (arts. 1 − 2), "ethics" (3 − 4),
"the individual" (5 − 6), "democratic society" (7 − 11), and "world community" (12 − 17).

"*First*: In the best sense, religion may inspire dedication to the
highest ethical ideals. The cultivation of moral devotion and creative
imagination is an expression of genuine 'spiritual' experience and
aspiration." The authors quickly add, however, that "traditional dogmatic or authoritarian religions ... do a disservice to the human
species." Further, they "find insufficient evidence for the existence of
a supernatural." For as "non-theists, we begin with humans not God,
nature not deity." Moreover, "we can discover no divine purpose or
providence for the human species." Hence, "no deity will save us; we
must save ourselves."

"*Second*: Promises of immortal salvation and fear of eternal dam-
nation are both illusory and harmful." Why? Because "they distract
humans from present concerns, from self-actualization, and from
rectifying social injustices." Modern science discredits belief in the
soul. "Rather, science affirms that the human species is an emergence
from natural evolutionary forces." Moreover, science has found "no
credible evidence that life survives the death of the body." Accordingly, man should spend his efforts looking after the welfare of this
life, not the next.

2. "Humanist Manifesto II," in *Humanist Manifestos I & II*, ed. Paul Kurtz (Buffalo:
Prometheus, 1973).

"*Third*: We affirm that moral values derive their source from human experience. Ethics is *autonomous* and *situational*, needing no theological or ideological sanction." Humanists base their system of values not on some transcendent "Other," but on human experience "here and now." Values have no suprahuman basis or goal.

"*Fourth: Reason and intelligence* are the most effective instruments that humankind possesses." For this there is no substitute. Neither faith nor passion will suffice. Indeed, humanists suggest that "the controlled use of scientific methods ... must be extended further in the solution of human problems." They claim that "critical intelligence, infused by a sense of human caring, is the best method that humanity has for resolving problems."

"*Fifth: The preciousness and dignity of the individual person is a central humanist value.*" That is, humanists allow for as much individual autonomy as is consistent with social responsibility. Accordingly, the framers of "Humanist Manifesto II" believe that "the possibilities of individual *freedom of choice* ... should be increased."

"Sixth: In the area of sexuality, we believe that intolerant attitudes, often cultivated by orthodox religions and puritanical cultures, unduly repress sexual conduct." The authors affirm "the right to birth control, abortion, and divorce." They also permit any form of "sexual behavior between consenting adults," for "a civilized society should be a *tolerant* one." In fact, they claim, "short of harming others or compelling them to do likewise, individuals should be permitted to express their sexual proclivities and pursue their life-styles as they desire."

"*Seventh*: To enhance freedom and dignity the individual must experience a full range of *civil liberties* in all societies." These liberties include "freedom of speech and the press, political democracy, the legal right of opposition to governmental policies, fair judicial process, religious liberty, freedom of association, and artistic, scientific, and cultural freedom, [as well as] recognition of an individual's right to die with dignity, euthanasia, and the right to suicide." Humanists also oppose the increasing invasion of individual privacy. This detailed list could well serve as a catalog of humanist values.

"*Eighth*: We are committed to an open and democratic society." Hence all persons should have a voice in developing their values and in choosing their goals. For "people are more important than decalogues, rules, proscriptions, or regulations." Here is manifest an opposition to divine moral law such as is found in the Ten Commandments.

"*Ninth*: The separation of church and state and the separation of ideology and state are imperatives." Humanists believe that the state "should not favor any particular religious bodies through the use of public monies, nor espouse a single ideology."

"*Tenth*: ... we need to democratize the economy and judge it by its responsiveness to human needs, testing results in terms of the common good." This means that the value of any economic system is to be judged on a utilitarian basis.

"*Eleventh*: The principle of moral equality must be furthered through elimination of all discrimination based on race, religion, sex, age, or national origin." Total elimination of discrimination, which would result in a more equitable distribution of wealth, would also involve a minimum guaranteed annual income, welfare to all who need it, and the right to a university education.

"*Twelfth*: We deplore the division of humankind on nationalistic grounds. We have reached a turning point in human history where the best option is to *transcend the limits of national sovereignty* and to move toward the building of a world community." This article calls for a supranational political entity which would allow for cultural diversity.

"*Thirteenth*: This world community must *renounce the resort to violence and force* as a method of solving international disputes." This article pronounces war obsolete, and claims it is a "planetary imperative" to reduce military spending.

"*Fourteenth*: The world community must engage in *cooperative planning* concerning the use of rapidly depleting resources ... and excessive population growth must be checked by international concord." For humanists, then, conservation is a moral value.

"*Fifteenth*: The problems of *economic growth and development* ... are worldwide in scope." Hence, "it is the moral obligation of the developed nations to provide ... massive technical, agricultural, medical, and economic assistance" to the underdeveloped nations. This is to be done through "an international authority that safeguards human rights."

"*Sixteenth: Technology is a vital key* to human progress and development." This article speaks against both indiscriminate condemnation of technology and the use of technology to "control, manipulate, or modify human beings without their consent."

"*Seventeenth*: We must expand communication and transportation across frontiers. Travel restrictions must cease." This article ends with the warning: "We must learn to live openly together or we shall perish together."

The conclusion of "Humanist Manifesto II" speaks out against "terror" and "hatred." It holds out the values of "reason and compassion" as well as "tolerance, understanding, and peaceful negotiation." It calls for "the highest commitment [i.e., to these values] of which we are capable," a commitment which "transcends ... church, state, party, class, or race." It is clear from this that humanists are calling for an ultimate commitment to transcendent moral values—a religious commitment.

A few general observations are in order. "Humanist Manifesto II" is stronger, more detailed, and less optimistic than "Humanist Manifesto I"; it is also less guarded in its use of *should* and in its call for an ultimate commitment. It is indeed a strong, urgent moral and religious call to all mankind. Like its predecessor, the second manifesto is atheistic, naturalistic, evolutionistic, socialistic, relativistic, and still optimistic that man can save himself. There is however, a much stronger international emphasis in the second statement.

The "Secular Humanist Declaration"

A third coalitional voice for secular humanism has been raised of late. In the secular humanist journal, *Free Inquiry,* a "Secular Humanist Declaration" recently appeared.[3] The signers of this document, including many who signed "Humanist Manifesto II," number, among others, novelist Isaac Asimov, situational ethicist Joseph Fletcher, philosophers Sidney Hook and Kai Nielsen, and psychologist B. F. Skinner.

The declaration espouses "democratic secular humanism." It is clear from the opening paragraphs that humanists see established religion as their chief enemy:

Regrettably, we are today faced with a variety of anti-secularist trends: the reappearance of dogmatic authoritarian religions; fundamentalist, literalist, and doctrinaire Christianity; a rapidly growing and uncom-

3. "A Secular Humanist Declaration," in *Free Inquiry,* Winter 1980 – 81, p. 3.

promising Moslem clericalism in the Middle East and Asia; the reassertion of orthodox authority by the Roman Catholic papal hierarchy; nationalistic religious Judaism; and the reversion to obscurantist religions in Asia.

The platform of these democratic secular humanists is as follows:

"1. *Free Inquiry.* The first principle of democratic secular humanism is its commitment to free inquiry. We oppose any tyranny over the mind of man, any efforts by ecclesiastical, political, ideological, or social institutions to shackle free thought."

"2. *Separation of Church and State.* Because of their commitment to freedom, secular humanists believe in the principle of the separation of church and state." In their view "any effort to impose an exclusive conception of Truth, Piety, Virtue, or Justice upon the whole of society is a violation of free inquiry."

"3. *The Ideal of Freedom.* . . . As democratic secularists, we consistently defend the ideal of freedom." The secular humanist concept of freedom includes not only freedom of conscience and belief from repressive ecclesiastical, political, and economic powers, but also "genuine political liberty, democratic decision-making based upon majority rule, and respect for minority rights and the rule of law."

"4. *Ethics Based on Critical Intelligence.* The secular humanist recognizes the central role of morality in human life." But "for secular humanists, ethical conduct is, or should be, judged by critical reason, and their goal is to develop autonomous and responsible individuals, capable of making their own choices in life based upon an understanding of human behavior." Although secular humanists are ostensibly opposed to absolutist morality, they maintain that "objective standards emerge, and ethical values and principles may be discovered, in the course of ethical deliberation."

"5. *Moral Education.* We believe that moral development should be cultivated in children and young adults . . . ; hence it is the duty of public education to deal with these values." Such values include "moral virtues, intelligence, and the building of character."

"6. *Religious Skepticism.* As secular humanists, we are generally skeptical about supernatural claims." While it is true that "we recognize the importance of religious experience: that experience that redirects and gives meaning to the lives of human [beings, we deny] that such experiences have anything to do with the supernatural."

In short, it is maintained that "secular humanists may be agnostics, atheists, rationalists, or skeptics, but [that there is] insufficient evidence for the claim that some divine purpose exists for the universe." Also, it is maintained that men and women are free and responsible for their own destinies and that they cannot look to any transcendent Being for salvation.

"7. *Reason.* We view with concern the current attack by non-secularists on reason and science." Although secular humanists deny reason and science can solve all human problems, they do affirm that they "know of no better substitute for the cultivation of human intelligence."

"8. *Science and Technology.* We believe the scientific method, though imperfect, is still the most reliable way of understanding the world. Hence, we look to the natural, biological, social, and behavioral sciences for knowledge of the universe and man's place within it."

"9. *Evolution.*" This article deplores the heavy attack religious fundamentalists are making on evolution. While denying that evolution is an "infallible principle," secular humanists believe it "is supported so strongly by the weight of evidence that it is difficult to reject it." Accordingly, they say, "we deplore the efforts by fundamentalists (especially in the United States) to invade the science classrooms, requiring that creationist theory be taught to students and requiring that it be included in biology textbooks." Secular humanists consider this "a serious threat both to academic freedom and to the integrity of the educational process."

"10. *Education.* In our view, education should be the essential method of building humane, free, and democratic societies." The aims of education include "the transmission of knowledge; the training for occupations, careers, and democratic citizenship; and the encouragement of moral growth." Secular humanists also envision the broader task of embarking on "a long-term program of public education and enlightenment concerning the relevance of the secular outlook to the human condition."

The declaration concludes with the plea that "democratic secular humanism is too important for human civilization to abandon." It decries contemporary orthodox religion as "anti-science, anti-freedom, anti-human," pointing out that "secular humanism places trust in human intelligence rather than in divine guidance." It ends by deploring "the growth of intolerant sectarian creeds that foster hatred."

It may seem surprising that this declaration appeared so soon after "Humanist Manifesto II" (only eight years later), especially since many of the same men signed both and much of the declaration is similar to the manifestos before it. With previous humanist statements it stresses naturalism, evolutionism, and man's ability to save himself, as well as common humanistic ethical commitments such as freedom, toleration, and critical intelligence.

However, the "Secular Humanist Declaration" does have some distinctives of its own. In fact, the most significant aspects of this declaration are those areas in which it differs from previous efforts. First of all, these secular humanists wish to be called democratic secular humanists. The stress on democracy is evident throughout. Second, nowhere do they claim to be religious humanists as do the authors of the prior manifestos. This is particularly strange, since humanists have pleaded for recognition as a religious group and since humanism has even been defined as a religion by the United States Supreme Court (*Torcaso* v. *Watkins*, 1961). Indeed, the declaration could be justly characterized as antireligious, for it particularly attacks the recent trend toward more conservative religious beliefs. The bulk of the declaration, in fact, seems to be a reaction against recent trends contrary to secular humanism. Finally, one cannot help but notice a strange inconsistency in that the declaration affirms academic freedom and yet insists that scientific creationism not be allowed in public-school science classes (see p. 93, n. 9).

Common Elements in Secular Humanism

A study of the "Humanist Manifestos I and II," the "Secular Humanist Declaration," and other writings of prominent secular humanists reveals a common core of beliefs amid the many diversities. There seem to be at least five common beliefs.

First, *nontheism* is common to all forms of secular humanism. Many secular humanists deny the existence of God altogether, but all deny the need for a God or a Creator of the world. Thus secular humanists are joined in opposing the traditional theism of such historic religions as Christianity, Judaism, and Islam.

Second, *naturalism* is an essential belief of secular humanism. This follows from its denial of theism. For if there is no supernatural Creator then there are no supernatural acts such as creation and the resurrection of Christ. Everything in the universe is thus explainable in terms of natural laws alone.

Third, *evolutionism* is the secular humanist's way of explaining origins. This too follows logically from the denial of a Creator. For either the universe and living things originated by means of the intervention of a supernatural Creator, or they evolved by purely natural means. Thus, denying the Creator leaves the secular humanist with the necessity of accepting some form of naturalistic evolution.

Fourth, *ethical relativism* unites secular humanists, for they have a distaste for absolutes. There are no God-given moral values; man decides his own values. These man-chosen ethical standards are subject to change and relative to different social situations. Since there is no absolute basis for values (in God) there are no absolute values to be received from God.

Fifth, *human self-sufficiency* is a central tenet. Not all secular humanists are utopian, but all do believe man is capable of solving his own problems without divine help. Not all secular humanists believe the race is immortal, but all hold that man's survival depends on himself. Not all believe that science and technology are the means of saving mankind, but all do believe that human reason and secular education are the only hope if the race is to endure.

10

The Helpful Emphases of Secular Humanism

Secular humanism has made many positive contributions to human life. In this chapter we will briefly mention several areas in which these contributions have been made. We have not attempted to be comprehensive or detailed, since in the first seven chapters we have expounded secular humanists' views and goals at length.

Ethical Contributions

Many of the moral principles of humanism are commendable; in fact, a number of them are held by Christians as well. Because of this it is inaccurate to speak of humanism as being in total opposition to Christianity. For, as we discussed earlier, there is a sense in which it is appropriate to speak of Christian humanism. Not that man is ultimate or infinite in value, but that the Infinite has given man intrinsic value.[1] Hence, to affirm human value is good. Man does make a significant contribution to the good in the world. On this both the secular humanist and the Christian are in agreement. Moreover, when viewed from a Christian perspective, humanism has made many positive ethical contributions, especially in the areas of moral education, freedom, and toleration.

1. See pp. 95 – 107.

Moral Education

Secular humanists speak of a right to education.[2] The "Secular Humanist Declaration" states, "We believe that moral development should be cultivated in children and young adults . . . ; hence it is the duty of public education to deal with these values."[3] Many Christians have long spoken out against what they view as an amoral public-school system which teaches no positive moral values. On this point there is agreement between secular humanist and Christian. Similarly, the tenth article of the declaration proclaims that "the aims of education are many: the transmission of knowledge . . . and democratic citizenship; and the encouragement of moral growth." Here too we find a worthy goal. Like Christians, then, secular humanists realize that an amoral education is surely not desirable.

Freedom

One of the points most persistently made by secular humanists is the need for freedom of the individual. In "Humanist Manifesto II" they declare, "To enhance freedom and dignity the individual must experience a full range of *civil liberties* in all societies."[4]

Contrary to a myth popular among many American Christians, most of the nation's founding fathers were *not* evangelical Christians. The Pilgrims were, of course, but they lived 150 years before the Declaration of Independence. Actually our nation's founders were largely humanistic (or deistic).[5] Some prominent men in early American history were even anti-Christian. Thomas Paine, for example, launched a bitter attack on Christianity in his book *The Age of Reason.* There were few evangelical Christians among the signers of the Declaration of Independence, John Witherspoon being a notable exception. And when George Washington was asked if the United States was a Christian country, he replied that "the Government of the United States of America is not in any sense founded on the

2. "Humanist Manifesto I," in *Humanist Manifestos I & II,* ed. Paul Kurtz (Buffalo: Prometheus, 1973), art. 11.
3. "A Secular Humanist Declaration," *Free Inquiry,* Winter 1980 − 81, art. 5.
4. "Humanist Manifesto II," art. 7.
5. A deist is one who believes in a Creator but generally denies the supernatural beyond that point; he might be called a theist on his way to becoming an atheist. The more radical deists are basically secular humanists without the courage (or will) to deny God.

Christian religion."[6] It is these early humanists who saw to it that our nation is committed to "life, liberty and the pursuit of happiness."

Along with political freedom secular humanists have strongly urged academic freedom. The "Secular Humanist Declaration" says that "the first principle of democratic secular humanism is its commitment to free inquiry. We oppose any tyranny over the mind of man."[7] A student of history can readily see that religion has often stifled freedom of thought. This is true of Islam and of Christianity, both Protestant and Catholic. Religious wars, persecution, the Ku Klux Klan, the Crusades, and the Inquisition have been a tragic testimony to the inhumanity perpetrated by religious people in the name of religion.

Secular humanists are to be commended for their goal to "defend the ideal of freedom, not only freedom of conscience and belief. . . , but genuine political liberty . . . and respect for minority rights and the rule of law."[8]

Toleration

One of the key words of the secular humanists is *toleration*. They rightly insist that "a civilized society should be a *tolerant* one."[9] "Live and let live" is their motto. This means that the minority has the right to differ from the majority. It also implies that all persons have a duty to respect those who differ from them—a duty not always performed by religious devotees. Tolerance also entails the renunciation of persecution, retaliation, and all forms of hatred. The conclusion of "Humanist Manifesto II" holds out the values of "tolerance, understanding, and peaceful negotiations." Surely secular humanists are to be lauded for professing these principles.

Our list of the virtues of secular humanism is not intended to be exhaustive. Those we have mentioned, which aim at countering racism, hatred, injustice, and inhumanity, will serve to highlight the point that humanism has offered many noble and valuable moral principles for mankind. Indeed, secular humanists have called on all of us for "the highest commitment [to morals] of which we are

6. Quoted in "Deism," in *The Encyclopedia of Philosophy*, ed. Paul Edwards (New York: Macmillan, 1967), vol. 2, p. 334.
7. "Secular Humanist Declaration," art. 1.
8. Ibid., art. 3.
9. "Humanist Manifesto II," art. 6.

capable," a commitment which "transcends ... church, state, party, class, or race."[10]

Political Goals

Besides the ethical considerations we have just discussed—the emphasis on moral education, freedom and toleration—secular humanists have pursued some idealistic political goals for society.

World Peace

Secular humanists generally repudiate war as a means of settling human disputes. Their pursuit of peace is persistent. They insist that "this world community must *renounce the resort to violence and force* as a method of solving international disputes." They say that "war is obsolete," and that "it is a planetary imperative to reduce military spending."[11] Despite the unrealism one senses here, there is nonetheless a most commendable idealism. War is evil, and peace should be pursued. As the apostle Paul put it in Romans, "If it is possible, as far as it depends on you, live at peace with everyone" (12:18).

Elimination of Poverty

There is a "war" secular humanists are waging: it is a war on poverty. Since this is a worldwide problem, secular humanists insist that "it is the moral obligation of the developed nations to provide ... massive technical, agricultural, medical, and economic assistance" to the underdeveloped nations.[12] While there is often disagreement (even among humanists) as to the best means of implementing such a program, nevertheless the goal of eliminating poverty is most commendable.

World Unity

In order to achieve world peace and elimination of poverty, humanists have often called for a unified world—not one that stifles individuality, creativity, or freedom, but one where there are equality

10. Ibid., conclusion.
11. Ibid., art. 13.
12. Ibid., art. 15.

and security for all and political oppression for none. Secular humanists are often in the forefront of supranational efforts to achieve such goals. They insist that "the world community must engage in *cooperative planning* concerning the use of rapidly depleting resources."[13] They add, "We must expand communication and transportation across frontiers." And then they proceed to issue a warning: "We must learn to live openly together or we shall perish together."[14] Many secular humanists see one world government as the only way to achieve this desired world unity. "Humanist Manifesto II" states, "We have reached a turning point in human history where the best option is to *transcend the limits of national sovereignty* and to move toward building of a world community."[15]

The Encouragement of Religious Attitudes

Secular humanists are far from irreligious. Many commend religion, and most call for and express a distinctly religious commitment (this will be discussed more fully in chapter 13).

The Call for a Humanistic Religion

Some secular humanists have started humanistic religions. Auguste Comte even installed himself as high priest of one of these sects. Most humanists frown on this kind of activity, although many call for a humanistic religion. In the preamble of "Humanist Manifesto I" the authors call themselves religious humanists and insist that "to establish such a religion is a major necessity of the present." In John Dewey's pragmatic humanism we even find a tendency to use the term *God*. Erich Fromm uses the word *God* to represent the highest and noblest aspects of human nature. The religious urge within humanism is generally not institutionalized; however, the Unitarian Universalist Association is a distinctly humanistic denomination.

Religious Commitment

Many humanists who refrain from using the term *God* have made a religious commitment to an ideal, goal, or ultimate. As we noted

13. Ibid., art. 14.
14. Ibid., art. 17.
15. Ibid., art. 12.

on page 118, some secular humanists call for the highest possible commitment to a system of values that transcends the human race. Huxley speaks of deeply religious, even mystical experiences.[16] The frequent use of terms such as *should*, *must*, and *imperative* reveals the religious fervor of secular humanism. In short, although most humanists prefer to live without the traditional concept of God, they do not wish to forsake all that is God-like. Many take a devoutly ethical and religious stance. To borrow John Dewey's distinction: they oppose religion but usually not the religious.[17]

Dialectical Contributions

Secular humanism plays an important dialectical or counterbalancing role in society. No open-minded, well-informed person can fail to see that there exist in human society narrow, radical, and prejudiced religious groups who would deny others many of the freedoms they themselves enjoy. History shows that humanists have often kept these extremists in check.

It was a narrow ecclesiastical authority which kept back scientific progress and condemned Galileo. The Crusades and the Inquisition were carried out in the name of Christianity. The Ku Klux Klan considers itself a devoutly religious organization. Right-wing Muslim countries have robbed many persons of civil and religious liberties. And it was not only unbelievers who perpetrated the Holocaust; many professing Christians contributed to the evil done to the Jews. In many cases, if humanists and their ideals did not counter these forces, society would experience even worse extremes. Humanism has thus played a vital role in making our world a more humane place. For this it is to be commended.

Cultural Improvements

Humanists have enriched our world a great deal by their cultural and aesthetic achievements in such areas as art, education, and

16. See pp. 11 – 20.
17. See pp. 48 – 58.

drama.[18] Humanists like Mortimer Adler have done much to advance the cause of learning. The Aspen Center for Humanistic Studies has made a significant impact on American culture. Furthermore, many advances in science and technology are the result of humanistic efforts. And UNESCO has influenced the whole world through its philanthropic programs.

Secular humanists have staffed many positions in American higher education. And through the philosophy of John Dewey secular humanism has left its mark on almost all Americans. In brief, this world is not only freer because of humanism, it is more beautiful, more advanced scientifically, and more variegated culturally.

Secular humanists have made significant contributions to many areas of human life. Ethically, they have advocated many important virtues such as freedom and tolerance. Politically, humanists have worked for peace and equality and against poverty and racism. Religiously, they often exemplify an ultimate commitment to their values and ideals. In the dialectic of history secular humanists have often served as a helpful corrective to narrow, prejudiced religions. And they have culturally and aesthetically enriched human life in many ways. For all of this and more we commend the secular humanists.

18. See pp. 83 – 94.

11

The Scientific Inadequacies of Secular Humanism

Secular humanists have always looked to science and technology to provide the solutions to man's problems:

> Using technology wisely, we can control our environment, conquer poverty, markedly reduce disease, extend our life-span, significantly modify our behavior, alter the course of human evolution and cultural development, unlock vast new powers, and provide humankind with unparalleled opportunity for achieving an abundant and meaningful life.[1]

Indeed, many secular humanists have long believed that science, not God or religion, is the means of man's salvation. "No deity will save us; we must save ourselves," they declare. How? "Reason and intelligence are the most effective instruments that humankind possess."

Recently secular humanists have tempered their enthusiastic hope that salvation will come through science, but they nonetheless continue to affirm that "the scientific method, though imperfect, is still the most reliable way of understanding the world. Hence, we look to the natural, biological, social, and behavioral sciences for knowledge of the universe and man's place in it."[2]

---

1. "Humanist Manifesto II," in *Humanist Manifestos I & II*, ed. Paul Kurtz (Buffalo: Prometheus, 1973), p. 14.
2. "Humanist Manifesto I," p. 5.

The Conflict Between Secular Humanists and Christians

In most areas there is little significant conflict between the scientific views of secular humanists and the scientific views of Christians. Basically, both groups agree that the physical universe operates by natural laws and that knowledge of these laws is helpful in understanding how it operates. For instance, Christian and humanistic scientists accept all the laws of physics, including the laws of thermodynamics and gravity. The real conflict does not have to do with the *operation* but with the *origination* of the universe and life. Secular humanists argue for a naturalistic explanation, while Christians argue for a supernatural one. The conflict is focused in three areas: (1) the origin of the universe, (2) the origin of first life, and (3) the origin of new life forms (including man). Figure 1 summarizes the two opposing views.

Figure 1 Origins

	Natural Explanation (Humanistic)	Supernatural Explanation (Christian)
Universe	Eternal	Created
First Life	Spontaneously generated	Specially created
New Life Forms	Evolved	Specially created

Secular humanists clearly deny creation and a Creator. In their first manifesto (1933) they declared, "We are convinced that the time has passed for theism, deism, modernism, and the several varieties of 'new thought.' "[3] Furthermore, "humanists regard the universe as self-existent and not created." Recently they reaffirmed their denial of God and the supernatural:

We find that traditional views of the existence of God either are meaningless, have not yet been demonstrated to be true, or are tyrannically exploitative. Secular humanists may be agnostics, atheists, rationalists,

3. Ibid., p. 8.

or skeptics, but they find insufficient evidence for the claim that some divine purpose exists for the universe.[4]

Secular humanists also have a naturalistic view of the origin of living things. "Humanism believes that man is part of nature and that he has emerged as the result of a continuous process."[5] Currently there is a note of caution in the secular humanists' affirmation of naturalistic evolution, but they have shown no willingness to give the theory up.[6] They still believe that a naturalistic, evolutionary view of origins is scientific. By contrast, Christians hold that belief in creation and a Creator is scientific.

The History of the Conflict

Most of the famous people in the early years of modern science were creationists. They believed in the supernatural origin of the universe and of life. Included among them are:

Johannes Kepler (1571 – 1630)	Celestial mechanics, physical astronomy
Blaise Pascal (1623 – 1662)	Hydrostatics
Robert Boyle (1627 – 1691)	Chemistry, gas dynamics
Nicolaus Steno (1638 – 1687)	Stratigraphy
Isaac Newton (1642 – 1727)	Calculus, dynamics
Michael Faraday (1791 – 1867)	Magnetic theory
Charles Babbage (1792 – 1871)	Computer science
Louis Agassiz (1807 – 1873)	Glacial geology, ichthyology
James Young Simpson (1811 – 1870)	Gynecology
Gregor Mendel (1822 – 1884)	Genetics
Louis Pasteur (1822 – 1895)	Bacteriology
Lord Kelvin (1824 – 1907)	Energetics, thermodynamics

4. "A Secular Humanist Declaration," *Free Inquiry,* Winter 1980 – 81, p. 5.
5. "Humanist Manifesto I," p. 8.
6. "A Secular Humanist Declaration," p. 6.

Joseph Lister (1827 – 1912)	Antiseptic surgery
James Clerk Maxwell (1831 – 1879)	Electrodynamics, statistical thermodynamics
William Ramsay (1852-1916)	Isotopic chemistry

In general, scientists before 1860 tended to be creationists. Sir Isaac Newton's statement about the origin of the universe is typical:

> This most beautiful system of the sun, planets, and comets, could only proceed from the counsel and dominion of an intelligent and powerful Being. And if the fixed stars are the centres of other like systems, these, being formed by the like wise counsel, must be all subject to the dominion of One.[7]

After Charles Darwin published *The Origin of Species* (1859), there was a radical change. His chief purpose was to present a naturalistic explanation of the origin of various species. In the last paragraph Darwin was careful to note that he was not attempting to give a naturalistic explanation of the origin of the first living thing(s). Indeed, he wrote, "There is grandeur in this view of life, with its several powers, having been originally breathed by the Creator into a few forms or into one."[8] Darwin, then, did not present a naturalistic explanation of the first created life or of the universe. Ultimately, however, this point of view became dominant.

The naturalistic view of the origin of the universe has posed some difficulties. One problem lies in reconciling it with the second law of thermodynamics, which affirms that the usable energy of the universe is running down—a situation that seems to point to a beginning (see p. 135). But astronomer Fred Hoyle has offered a solution: his "steady state" theory proposes that hydrogen atoms spontaneously come into existence. This keeps the universe from running down and thus explains how it could be eternal.

Another stumbling block to a totally naturalistic explanation of origins was Louis Pasteur's disproof of the spontaneous generation

7. Newton, *Mathematical Principles of Natural Philosophy*, trans. Andrew Motte, in Great Books of the Western World, ed. Robert Maynard Hutchins (Chicago: Encyclopedia Britannica, 1952), vol. 34, p. 369.

8. Darwin, *The Origin of Species*, in Great Books of the Western World, ed. Robert Maynard Hutchins (Chicago: Encyclopedia Britannica, 1952), vol. 49, p. 243.

of life. However, with the experiments of Dayton Miller and Harold Urey the naturalistic explanation became more credible. By passing an electrical discharge through certain gases, scientists are able to produce amino acids, the building blocks of life. From this it has been posited that in the "primeval sea" lightning could have caused nonliving chemicals to develop into the first life. The theory of evolution goes on to explain the development of life from there. This naturalistic approach stands in direct contrast to the views of many earlier scientists, who regarded the origin of the universe and life as supernatural.

Basic Scientific Principles

Before we more thoroughly compare the naturalistic and supernaturalistic views of origin, we must have a basic understanding of the nature of science. Scientists do not universally agree on every aspect of the scientific method. But they do agree on a few essentials. First, science involves *observation* of the physical world. It is based on observations which can be made, not merely by one scientist, but by any scientists who wish to study the phenomenon in question.

Second, science involves *repetition*. Unless an event can be repeated it is considered an anomaly. Since an event observed by only one person and/or at only one time has not been observed and tested by anyone else, science remains justifiably skeptical of "private" observations. No old laws are revised or new laws formulated on the basis of only one observation. Hence repetition is a second fundamental characteristic of science. (There are, of course, other elements of the scientific method—such as the canons of the inductive procedure outlined by Francis Bacon and developed by John Stuart Mill. But these complement the other principles.)

The two fundamental principles of science, observation and repetition, are absolutely crucial when we are dealing with phenomena of the present world. However, when we are dealing with origins *neither observation nor repetition applies*. This is so for the simple reason that there were no observers of the origin of the universe and of living things. Furthermore, the unique events of origin cannot be repeated. They happened once, and that was in the unobserved past. Thus the events of the origin of the universe and of life simply are not available for observation and testing in the present. This means that in the strict sense of the word *science* (involving observed and repeatable events) there can be no science of origins. We simply do not have any direct access to the original events by which we can test our theories about them.

But the lack of direct access to the events of origin does not mean that there can be no scientific approach to them. For there are several other principles of science which apply to past events we cannot observe.

First, the principle of *causality* is operative for past events. It affirms that there is a cause (a necessary and sufficient condition) for every event. Events do not occur without causes.

Second, there is the principle of *uniformity* (or analogy). The broadest formulation of this principle is that "the present is the key to the past." That is, what we observe in the present can be used to understand what took place but was not observed in the past. Thus while the past cannot be known directly, it can be understood indirectly by analogy with the present.

Third, there is the principle of *consistency.* Any scientific model that one constructs of the past must be consistent with all other elements of one's scientific views. Anything contradictory to those views must be rejected.

Fourth, there is the principle of *comprehensiveness.* A good model explains all available data. Anomalies will persist, but no indisputable data can be neglected in theory construction. All other things being equal, the most comprehensive view is judged to be the best one.

Now with the aid of these principles we shall see that secular humanism's naturalistic view of the origin of the universe and of life is scientifically inadequate.

Inadequacy of the Naturalistic View

The Origin of the Universe

The principle of causality

Every event has an adequate cause. This is one of the most fundamental of all scientific principles. Combining the principle of causality with scientific evidence for a beginning of the universe brings one face to face with the supernatural. Included in this evidence is the second law of thermodynamics, which holds that in a closed system (such as the whole universe)[9] the amount of *usable* energy is decreasing; that is, energy is being used up (transformed into heat). So the universe is running down. But if the universe is running down, then it is not eternal. For if the universe were eternal (i.e., had no beginning), it would have run down by now—unless, of course, there were an infinite amount of energy. But since the usable energy is being exhausted, it is not infinite. So then, the universe must have had a beginning. And since, according to the principle of causality, *every* event has a cause, it would follow that the beginning of the universe had a cause.

Other evidence has led most contemporary astronomers to conclude that the universe began with a Big Bang (that is, with a violent eruption that created matter). The astrophysicist Robert Jastrow writes,

> No explanation other than the Big Bang has been found for the fireball radiation. The clincher, which has convinced almost the last doubting Thomas, is that the radiation discovered by Penzias and Wilson has exactly the pattern of wavelengths expected for the light and heat produced in a great explosion. Supporters of the Steady State theory have tried desperately to find an alternative explanation, but they have failed.[10]

This evidence is not a happy result for the secular humanist. As Jastrow notes,

> For the scientist who has lived by his faith in the power of reason, the story ends like a bad dream. He has scaled the mountains of ignorance; he is about to conquer the highest peak; as he pulls himself over the final rock, he is greeted by a band of theologians who have been sitting there for centuries.[11]

One thing is clear: it is certainly in accord with scientific principles to affirm a Creator of the universe. And those who like the secular humanists do not affirm a Creator are ignoring basic principles of science.

9. If the universe were "open" to receiving energy from some force beyond it, this would itself be a form of supernaturalism.

10. Robert Jastrow, *God and the Astronomers* (New York: W. W. Norton, 1978), p. 15.

11. Ibid., p. 116.

The principle of uniformity (analogy)

According to the principle of uniformity, "the present is the key to the past." If so, then we can argue that the universe has a Creator. For there is no modern-day evidence of random forces which could have brought the immense complexities of the universe into being.

Some insist that the principle of uniformity really argues against creation. They note that everything we observe today is the result of a gradual process and that the universe does not manifest abrupt beginnings. Hence, they argue that if "the *processes* of the present are the key to the past," we must reject the concept of an abrupt creation of the universe.

On several counts, however, this reasoning is not sound. First of all, even in the most common naturalistic explanation of the origin of the universe—the Big Bang theory—there is an abrupt event in the past which is not occurring today. Second, according to all naturalistic explanations of the origin of life there is an abrupt, singular event of the past—spontaneous generation, which causes the non-living to become living—which is not occurring in the present. And even if scientists do succeed in creating life, it will take intelligence to do so.

Finally, the naturalist has made an error in his formulation of the principle of uniformity. He has reworded the principle from "the present is the key to the past" to "the *processes* of the present are the key to events of the past." When the naturalist's formulation of the principle is put in more complete form, his error is even more evident: "The *repeated* processes of the present are the key to unique *unrepeated* events of the past." Obviously we have here a basic equivocation in the naturalist's understanding of the principle of uniformity. He is comparing repeatable processes of the present with unrepeatable events of the past.

The naturalist is in fact confusing two fundamentally different kinds of scientific principles—principles of *origination* and principles of *operation*. Let us restate the principle of uniformity in this context: "The *operation* of the universe in the present is the key to the *operation* of the universe in the past." The naturalist has incorrectly interpreted this to mean that "the *operation* of the universe in the present is the key to the *origination* of the universe in the past."

Theist and naturalist agree on the basic operational laws of the universe. They agree that these laws apply to both the present and past *operations* of the universe. However, the theist disagrees with the secular humanist's contention that laws of *operation* can adequately account for the *origination* of the universe and living things. For example, the laws by which a car operates (inertia, gravity, tension, etc.) cannot actually produce a car. A car operates by nonrational natural laws, but it originates through intelligence.

Similarly, good literature follows the laws of good grammar. But these laws of grammar never by themselves produce a Shakespearean sonnet.[12] It takes intelligence for that. Hence the principle of uniformity rightly understood does not argue against creation but for it. For if the laws of origin in the present are a key to the events of origin in the past, then it is certainly scientific to conclude that it took intelligence to produce the universe of living things.

The principles of consistency and comprehensiveness

Positing an intelligent Creator of the universe is *consistent* with all we observe in the present, for we observe that intelligence is the cause of our complex systems of information. Furthermore, the idea of an intelligent Creator accords with the principle of *comprehensiveness*, since an intelligent Creator can account for all the data of the physical universe. Even the so-called random events are part of some overall order. Although Werner Heisenberg's principle of uncertainty (actually, unpredictability) says we do not know where a given subatomic particle will be at a given time, we are assured that it has a regular part in an overall orderly pattern. Likewise, the molecules of carbon dioxide we exhale will take a random course throughout the room. However, there is a good overall purpose for this. If they did not bounce around randomly, we would be inhaling too many of them right back into our lungs instead of the necessary amounts of oxygen. Perhaps not every event in nature has an identifiable specific purpose which reflects an intelligent Creator, but the overall pattern does. Each mysterious particular is explainable—at least in principle—in terms of that overall order.[13]

12. See the quote by Michael Polanyi on p. 144.

13. Although it is our purpose here to deal with only the physical world, the same can be said of the moral world. That is, all moral events (including evil ones) can be explained as the result of the good, intelligent choice by the Creator to create human beings who can make intelligent and good choices of their own. Of course, humans can also make choices that are not so good and intelligent; evil results from these poor choices. (For further discussion of this see my *Roots of Evil* [Grand Rapids: Zondervan, 1980].)

There are other aspects of the comprehensive picture of the universe which are not adequately explained by the naturalists. There is the evidence of the second law of thermodynamics that the universe is running down. The naturalistic notion of an eternal universe is hard to square with the fact that it is running down. For, as we have already seen, if the universe were eternal (i.e., had no beginning), it would have run down a long time ago.

Therefore we can conclude that a creationist view is at least as scientific as the naturalistic view. In fact, we can reasonably conclude that the supernaturalistic view is more scientific than a purely naturalistic explanation. For all naturalistic explanations, if they are to square with the principle of causality, must posit eternal matter. But there is no evidence that matter (or energy) is eternal. The actual amount of energy is constant (first law of thermodynamics), but the *usable* amount is running down (second law). Thus there is overwhelming observational evidence against any purely naturalistic explanation, whether it be the "Big Bubble" theory of J. Richard Gott,[14] the "steady state" theory Hoyle proposed, or any kind of oscillating-universe theory. They are all purely speculative hypotheses without evidence and contravene the universally confirmed second law of thermodynamics.

The Origin of First Life

The principle of causality

A cause is both a necessary and sufficient condition. But we have no evidence of even the necessary condition for life to appear by spontaneous generation. There is no evidence that any primeval pond with the right concentration of chemical elements ever existed on earth. Some scientists have frankly acknowledged this. J. Brooks and G. Shaw admit that "in fact no such materials have been found anywhere on earth."[15] William Day adds this illuminating comment:

> A curious flaw of human nature is to permit the imagery of a catchy phrase to shape one's reasoning. Haldane's hot dilute soup became

14. According to Gott, an astronomer at Princeton University, the present universe is simply a bubble in an apparently eternal sea of energy.

15. J. Brooks and G. Shaw, *The Origin and Development of Living Systems* (New York: Academic, 1973), p. 396.

"primordial soup," a feature that has been popularized for nearly fifty years without geologic evidence that it ever existed.[16]

Random force is not an adequate cause for the production of life. For random force has a diffusive and rounding effect on nature, not an ordering and directive effect as is needed to produce life. Wind and water scatter dust and round off rocks. But the sharp features on an arrowhead are caused by an intelligent being. Hurricanes raging through lumber yards do not produce new homes. Falling confetti at a parade does not spell out a hero's name. It takes intelligence to produce new homes and to arrange pieces of paper to spell out a name. Similarly, it would be scientifically foolish to posit anything less than an intelligent cause of first life in the universe.

The principle of uniformity

If present observations are the key to the past origination of life, then creation by an intelligent Being is a more adequate scientific alternative than is spontaneous generation. This is so for several reasons. First, there is absolutely no observational evidence that life ever arises spontaneously from the nonliving. The results of Louis Pasteur's experiments still stand unchallenged. Spontaneous generation of life from the nonliving never occurs.

Second, in the laboratory experiments where chemicals (such as amino acids) essential to life are produced from nonliving gases, *intelligent intervention (manipulation) is crucial to the success of the experiments.* For example, if the experiments are to succeed, the chemicals used must be in a form about one million times more concentrated than they occur naturally anywhere on earth.[17] This requires some sort of intervention.

Third, the laws of physics and chemistry alone cannot account for the origin of life, but there is a regularly observed power that can help account for it. This power is the same scientific power used in the attempt to create life. It is *intelligence.*

Even the simplest form of life is incredibly complex, containing as much information as a volume of the *Encyclopedia Britannica.* We

16. William Day, *Genesis on Planet Earth: The Search for Life's Beginning* (East Lansing, Mich.: House of Talos, 1979), pp. 231 – 232.

17. I am indebted for these observations to Charles Thaxton, who has lectured on this topic for a number of years and has coauthored a forthcoming book on the origin of life.

observe intelligence regularly producing such information. But we never observe an encyclopedia resulting from an explosion in a printing shop! We observe that blowing hard on one's alphabet cereal merely produces a mess. Yet using intelligence to put these letters together can convey very complex information. Since present observations indicate intelligence is necessary to produce an encyclopedia or to put letters together coherently, it is reasonable to conclude that intelligence was necessary to bring life into being.

The principles of consistency and comprehensiveness

Is there any evidence that is inconsistent with positing an intelligent cause of first life? Some have suggested that the laws of probability dictate that given enough time even the virtually impossible becomes inevitable. However, even naturalistic scientists admit that the odds are infinitesimal for even the simplest form of life to arise by chance. Harold F. Blum writes,

> The chances of forming tripeptides would be about one hundredth that of forming dipeptides, and the probability of forming a polypeptide of only ten amino acids as units would be something like 10^{-20}. *The spontaneous formation of a polypeptide of the size of the smallest known proteins seems beyond all probability.*[18]

One evolutionist has even said, "One has only to contemplate the magnitude of this task to concede that the spontaneous generation of a living organism is impossible.[19]

The statistical impossibility of spontaneous generation notwithstanding, naturalistic scientists continue to believe against all odds that it did happen. Most knowledgeable scientists, however, must agree with H. P. Yockey: "One must conclude that, contrary to the established and current wisdom, a scenario describing the genesis of life on earth by chance and natural causes which can be accepted on the basis of fact and not faith has not yet been written."[20]

Admitting the astronomical improbabilities of a chance beginning

18. Harold F. Blum, *Time's Arrow and Evolution* (Princeton, N.J.: Princeton University, 1955), p. 163 (emphasis added).
19. George Wald, "The Origin of Life," in *Life: Origin and Evolution* (San Francisco: W. H. Freeman, 1979), p. 48.
20. H. P. Yockey, "A Calculation of the Probability of Spontaneous Biogenesis by Information Theory," *Journal of Theoretical Biology* 67 (1977): 396.

of life on earth, some have suggested life came from outer space. The atheist Fred Hoyle and his colleague, N. C. Wickramasinghe, set out to show that genetic material arriving on earth via meteorites could provide the raw material for the origin of terrestrial life.[21] They were startled by their own calculations. Given the billions of years accepted by most modern scientists, the odds for even the simplest form of life arising by this method (without the intervention of an intelligent Creator) were 1 in $10^{40,000}$! Since $10^{40,000}$ is more than the number of atoms in the whole universe, the odds that life originated from material arriving on meteorites would be like the chances of finding one particular atom in the whole universe, a needle in an astronomical haystack.

Some have suggested that allowing for enough time will solve the problem. George Wald writes, "Time is in fact the hero of the plot. . . . Given so much time, the 'impossible' becomes possible, the possible probable, and the probable virtually certain. One has only to wait: time itself performs miracles."[22] But there are several reasons that positing billions of years will not help the naturalistic explanation. First, time is already figured into the astronomical odds. Second, time combined with random force has never been observed to produce information such as is found in a living cell. Giving confetti more time to fall (by dropping it from an airplane) will not increase the chances of its spelling out a hero's name when it reaches the ground.[23] Actually, observations show that the longer the time of fall, the more random will be the dispersion of the confetti. And since what is presently observed is the key to what is unobserved in the past, we must conclude that it is unscientific to believe that even the simplest form of life arose without the intelligence of a Creator.

Not only is there no evidence to indicate that anything as complex as life arises by pure chance, but all the evidence indicates that nonlife never produces life. Pasteur's experiments long ago disproved spontaneous generation. So if spontaneous generation in the present is disproven, why do naturalistic scientists continue to believe it happened in the past? Is this not a violation of the principle that "the present is the key to the past"?

21. Fred Hoyle and N. C. Wickramasinghe, *Evolution from Space* (London: Dent, 1981), p. 24.

22. George Wald, "The Origin of Life," p. 48.

23. See A. E. Wilder-Smith, *Man's Origin, Man's Destiny* (Minneapolis: Bethany Fellowship, 1968), pp. 66 – 69.

Another aspect of the inadequacy of the naturalistic theory of origin is its inability to explain the appearance of complex life forms in the earliest rocks. The remains of life that we have from the Cambrian period are very complex forms which include most of the basic phyla.[24] In 1978 fully developed vertebrate fishes were discovered in Cambrian rocks.[25] Even if science can establish the existence of living organisms in the pre-Cambrian period—now a matter of dispute—the relatively sudden appearance of these highly complex little organisms is best explained by an intelligent Creator. There is no evidence to the contrary.

If the evidence is against spontaneous generation, why, then, do secular humanists persist in defending it? J. W. N. Sullivan provides a key in his book, *The Limitations of Science:* "But careful experiments, notably those of Pasteur, showed that this conclusion [that spontaneous generation could occur] was due to improper observation, and it became an accepted doctrine that life never arises except from life. So far as actual evidence goes, this is still the only possible conclusion. . . . But since it is a conclusion that seems to lead back to some supernatural creative act, it is a conclusion that scientific men find very difficult to accept."[26]

The Origin of New Life Forms

Now let us briefly apply these same scientific principles to the origin of new life forms. Secular humanists universally believe in some form of macroevolution, that is, that all present species evolved from early forms of life. Christians believe that God created all the basic forms of life. Evolutionists hold that all living things have a common ancestry; creationists hold a separate ancestry for different forms of life. Which view is more scientific?

The principle of causality

As was already noted, the only adequate cause for the origin of even the simplest form of life is an intelligent Creator. How much

24. Preston Cloud has said that not a single indisputable multicellular fossil has been found in pre-Cambrian rocks, which would seem to indicate rapid development of life in the Cambrian period. See "Pseudofossils: A Plea for Caution," *Geology* 1 (1973): 123.

25. See John E. Repetski, "A Fish from Upper Cambrian Strata," *Science* 200 (1978): 529.

26. J. W. N. Sullivan, *The Limitations of Science* (1933; repr. ed., New York: New American Library, 1956), p. 94.

more so is this true of the origin of higher, more complex forms of life! For if it takes intelligent intervention to make a simple one-cell organism (which contains as much genetic information as there is general knowledge in a volume of the *Encyclopedia Britannica*), how much more is intelligence necessary to produce something as complex as the human brain (which has more genetic information than all the facts contained in all the libraries of the world)! According to evolution the lower, less complex organisms gave rise to the higher, more complex forms *without the intervention of an intelligent Creator.* But nonintelligent random forces are not adequate to account for such macroleaps of "information transformation" (the changing of genetic codes to those of a more complex organism). Rather, each living thing has its own unique genetic-information center (DNA) which programs it to be the specific organism it is. Further, each living thing always generates another like itself.

There is strong evidence that the laws governing the lower organisms are not adequate to produce the higher organisms. As the famous philosopher of science Michael Polanyi notes,

> Accordingly, the operations of a higher level cannot be accounted for by the laws governing its particulars forming the lower level. You cannot derive a vocabulary from phonetics; you cannot derive the grammar of a language from its vocabulary; a correct use of grammar does not account for good style; and a good style does not provide the content of a piece of prose.[27]

If this is so, naturalistic evolution is ruled out. For there must be some higher intelligence to inform the higher organism to be a higher and not a lower organism.

Evolutionists sometimes attempt to explain that the higher information center was developed by random mutations (or mistakes) in the genetic code. But this too is an inadequate explanation. Any English teacher can confirm that random mistakes in a fourth-grader's poem never produce *Paradise Lost.* And the difference in the complexity of genetic information contained in higher and lower organisms is even greater than the difference in complexity between the poetry of a schoolchild and that of John Milton.

Evolutionists believe that genetic information can be transferred

27. Michael Polanyi, *The Tacit Dimension* (Routledge & Kegan Paul, 1966), p. 36.

from one form of life to another by random force. Not only is this
contrary to all observation, it would be magic. This is obvious in that
the naturalists have to appeal to chance mutations as the means of
macroevolution. The humanistic evolutionist Julian Huxley admitted
that the chances for the evolution of a horse are 1 in $1000^{1,000,000}$.
(This is the number *one* followed by three million zeroes or fifteen
hundred pages of nothing but zeroes!) He admitted that no one
would ever bet on anything so improbable.[28] Yet he persisted in
believing it *did* happen!

Even after probabilities are discussed, the question still remains
as to what might be an adequate *cause* of such an improbable event.
Huxley's answer was "natural selection." But this is inadequate for
several reasons. First, natural selection does not account for the
arrival of entirely new forms of life but only the *survival* of old ones
(by their ability to adapt to a new environment). Natural selection is
a *conserving* force for living things, not a *producing* force. Animals
sometimes lose organs or their functions, but natural selection has
never shown how entirely new functional organs can be produced.

Second, natural selection is only a descriptive law. It only describes
how the forces at work in nature preserve the species. One can still
ask *why* there is such an adaptability within the very nature of living
organisms which enables them to survive. The creationist's reply to
this question makes good sense: because God created them with this
tremendous ability to adapt to changing environments so as to preserve life.

The very least this discussion shows is that natural selection does
not cause macroevolutionary changes which result in entirely different kinds of organisms (such as a whale from a cow). It is only an
explanation of minor variations (or microevolutionary changes) within
a particular kind of organism which enable it to survive. The best
scientific explanation for the differences between lower and higher
forms of life is still an intelligent Creator.

The principle of uniformity

The principle of uniformity is hard on naturalistic evolution. For
in the present we never observe macroevolution occurring. Each kind
of living thing gives rise to its own kind. And even when scientists

28. Julian Huxley, *Evolution in Action* (New York: Harper and Brothers, 1953),
pp. 45 – 46.

try to change one species into another (as in the fruit-fly experiments of Francisco J. Ayala), the mutation is still of the same genus (*Drosophila*). Even the wing and eye mutations produced by intelligent interference of the scientists are not permanent. After a few generations the flies return to their original form.

Suppose, however, that scientists do succeed in producing an entirely new form of life by genetic manipulation. What will this prove? It will prove again that it takes intelligent intervention to produce higher forms of life—which is exactly what the creationists argue.

Even the Darwinian's famous peppered moths do not provide evidence for evolution. Before the Industrial Revolution in England there were many white moths. But as the revolution progressed, black moths came to predominate, since black ones could survive better on soot-covered objects. However, as even evolutionists admit,

> The (peppered moth) experiments beautifully demonstrate natural selection—or survival of the fittest—in action, but they do not show evolution in progress, for however the populations may alter in their content of light, intermediate, or dark forms, all the moths remain from beginning to end *biston betularia.*[29]

In fact, all present-day evidence supports the creationist's contention that one form of life never changes into an entirely different form—a cat never changes into a dog, nor a cow into a whale. So if the present is the key to the past, then we have no scientific reason to believe macroevolution happened in the past either.

At this point many evolutionists object by invoking the time factor. They argue that a few hundred years of scientific observation are not enough. Given a longer period of scientific observation, we might observe changes big enough to lend support to the theory of macroevolutionary changes occurring over millions of years. Time is the miracle-working hero of the evolutionary plot.

From a scientific point of view there are many problems with this argument. First, pleading for more time is an admission that hundreds of years of scientific observation have not given any support to the

---

29. L. Harrison Matthews, "Introduction," in Charles Darwin, *Origin of Species* (London: Dent, 1971), p. xi.

theory of macroevolution. In short, it is a confession that no supporting evidence has been observed. Second, time does not help but actually hinders the ability of random forces to produce new forms of life. Remember, allowing more time for confetti to randomly fall means it is less likely to spell out a hero's name when it reaches the ground. Third, the discovery of very early, yet highly complex forms of life (such as fish in the Cambrian period) contradicts the idea that evolution advanced by small, gradual changes. In fact, the evidence has forced many naturalistic evolutionists to admit that there must have been "leaps" in the evolutionary ascent. Stephen J. Gould's "punctuated equilibria" is such an admission. He claims evolution is not always gradual—like a ball rolling up a hill. Rather, it is more like a ball bouncing up a staircase.

How, we may ask, does a ball bounce *up* a staircase without some outside force directing it? Natural laws (like gravity) would demand that the ball bounce *down* the staircase. Further, each "stair" is a higher and more complex form of life. How does an organism attain this higher level by a sudden leap? Surely students would like to know how they can leap from kindergarten to a Ph.D. degree without any new input of information from the outside! And the leaps in the evolutionary ascent are even greater than this.

Another inadequacy of the naturalistic explanation is its inability to explain the sudden appearance of new life forms in the fossil record.[30] When life begins in the Cambrian period, it begins "suddenly" and "abundantly" like a great "explosion"—all words used by evolutionists. When new life forms appear, they begin suddenly with no transitional forms to tie them to lower forms. Some scientists have referred to these transitional elements as "missing links." This is misleading for two reasons. First, it assumes there is only one "chain" of life, which begs the whole question. Maybe there are many "chains"—one for each created kind. Second, even if we grant the "chain" image, it is not "links" that are missing; most of the "chain" is missing! Certainly we would not speak of missing links if we had only one link in Los Angeles, another in Chicago, and a third in New York. That would be more like a "missing chain." The evidence in the fossil record shows enormous gaps; for example, the gap between the cow and the whale (which many evolutionists believe evolved

---

30. Duane Gish, *Evolution? The Fossils Say No!* (San Diego: Creation-Life, 1972).

from the cow).[31] In fact, there is an utter lack of fossil evidence that the whale evolved from the cow! Fossil evidence for the macroleaps needed by evolution is not merely sparse, it is nonexistent.

The highly advertised cases of the coelacanth (a supposed link between fish and reptile) and the archaeopteryx (supposedly half bird, half reptile) do not qualify as true transitional forms. The archaeopteryx had perfectly feathered wings. It was a full-fledged bird! The fact that it has teeth does not mean it was a reptile. Other ancient birds had teeth, as do virtually all subclasses of vertebrates today. And the fact that the archaeopteryx had claws on its wings does not prove it was a reptile. Many modern birds have claws, including the young hoatzin of South America, the touraco of Africa, and the ostrich. Yet evolutionists do not suggest these are reptiles on their way to becoming birds!

In the case of the coelacanth, there is no evidence that its sturdy fins ever developed into legs and that this fish then became amphibious. The true amphibian has leg bones and a pelvic girdle firmly attached to the backbone. This structure enables the legs to support the body weight, and thus the amphibian is able to walk. The coelacanth does not have legs, but fins loosely attached with muscle. This structure cannot support the body and therefore the coelacanth cannot walk. Nor does the so-called walking catfish really walk; it slithers along on its belly. Furthermore, the coelacanth, once believed to be extinct for millions of years, has been found alive. It looks exactly like the fossils supposedly sixty million years old. And its fins are still fins; they have not developed into legs—even after sixty million years.

What the evolutionists must find to demonstrate their missing links are fossils with feathers and scales, or with fins and developed legs. These have not been found; in fact, no evidence from the past proves the existence of any true transitional fossils. Rather, evidence for missing links is totally missing. Whenever a new form of life appears in the fossil record it is complete and functional. The first bat was a bat, the first elephant was an elephant, and the first monkey was a monkey. A similar statement could be made of all species. The initial complexity of each species argues for an intelligent Creator.

If evolution were true there must have been billions of transitional

---

31. See the foldout "Whales of the World," in "Exploring the Lives of Whales," by Victor Scheffer, *National Geographic* (December, 1976), pp. 752 – 767.

fossils, and yet not one indisputable example has ever been found. Some experts have acknowledged this. One of the world's foremost paleontologists wrote in 1979,

> I fully agree with your comments on the lack of direct illustration of evolutionary transitions in my book. If I knew of any, fossil or living, I would certainly have included them. So, much as I should like to oblige you by jumping to the defense of gradualism, and fleshing out the transitions between the major types of animals and plants, I find myself a bit short of the intellectual justification necessary for the job.[32]

In other words, if he had known of any transitional fossils he would have gladly illustrated them in his book. But since there are none, he could not include them.

Later (1981) this same scientist said in a lecture:

> One of the reasons I started taking this anti-evolutionary or let's call it a non-evolutionary view, was last year I had a sudden realization for over twenty years I had thought I was working on evolution in some way. One morning I woke up and something had happened in the night and it struck me that I had been working on this stuff for twenty years and there was not one thing I knew about it. That's quite a shock to learn that one can be so misled so long.[33]

The principles of consistency and comprehensiveness

The foregoing discussion illustrates some basic inconsistencies in the thinking of evolutionists. First of all, they claim that the present is the key to the past, yet they can provide no evidence from the present for macroevolutionary changes. Second, they claim to base their view on evidence from the past as well, and yet the only evidence from the past (fossils) shows absolutely no grounds for macroevolution. Third, they admit the virtual impossibility of random formation of even simple life forms, and yet they believe that even the incredibly more complex higher forms resulted from random forces.

As to the principle of comprehensiveness, evolutionists have mani-

32. Colin Patterson, in a letter cited by William J. Guste, Jr., in the "Plaintiff's Pre-Trial Brief" for a recent Louisiana trial on creation and evolution (June 3, 1982).

33. Colin Patterson, "Evolutionism and Creationism," a speech given at the American Museum of Natural History (New York) on November 5, 1981.

fested an extraordinary agility in their attempts to explain *all* the data. New finds (or the lack thereof) have forced them to postulate *ad hoc* hypotheses that have occasioned admissions that the evolutionary theory is so all-inclusive that there would be no way to prove it false. Karl Popper concludes, "Darwinism is not a testable scientific theory, but a *meta-physical research programme.*"[34] Others have made similar admissions.[35] In brief, the general theory of evolution is so comprehensive it has no basic content. By explaining everything it really does not explain anything—at least not in a scientifically verifiable manner.[36]

Science is based on observations in the present. According to the principle of uniformity, these observations can be used as a key to understanding the past. This evidence together with the principles of causality, consistency, and comprehensiveness leads one to conclude that the secular humanist explanation of origins is scientifically inadequate. As a result of the lack of corroborating scientific evidence, humanistic explanations of origin have become a matter of faith. One writer put the humanists' embarrassment this way:

> With the failure of these many efforts science was left in the somewhat embarrassing position of having to postulate theories of living origins which it could not demonstrate. After having chided the theologian for his reliance on myth and miracle, science found itself in the unenviable position of having to create a mythology of its own: namely, the assumption that what, after long effort, could not be proved to take place today had, in truth, taken place in the primeval past.[37]

34. Karl Popper, *Unended Quest: An Intellectual Autobiography* (La Salle, Ill.: Open Court, 1976), p. 168 (emphasis added).

35. E.g., L. C. Birch and P. R. Ehrlich, "Evolutionary History and Population Biology," in *Nature*, April 1967, p. 351: "Our theory of evolution has become, as Popper described, one which cannot be refuted by any possible observations. Every conceivable observation can be fitted into it. It is thus 'outside of empirical science' but not necessarily false. No one can think of ways in which to test it. Ideas, either without basis or based on a few laboratory experiments carried out in extremely simplified systems, have attained currency far beyond their validity. They have become part of an evolutionary dogma accepted by most of us as part of our training."

36. Colin Patterson has said that the "explanatory value of the hypothesis of common ancestry is nil." He adds, "I feel that the effect of hypotheses of common ancestry in systematics has not been merely boring, not just a lack of knowledge, but I think it has been positively anti-knowledge." (See note 32 for bibliographical data.)

37. Loren Eisley, *The Immense Journey* (New York: Vintage, 1957), p. 199.

12

The Internal
Inconsistencies
of Secular Humanism

There are a number of ways fairly to evaluate a philosophy of life such as secular humanism. One method, which we will use in this chapter, is to examine the philosophy to see if its various claims are consistent, or if they in fact cancel each other.

There are two ways we will apply the test of consistency to secular humanism. First, we will examine whether the various kinds of humanism discussed in chapters 1 – 8 are compatible. Second, we will examine whether the basic common beliefs of secular humanism as set forth in its manifestos and declaration are consistent with each other.

Inconsistencies Between the Various Kinds of Humanism

Nonreligious versus Religious Humanism

One can be a humanist and still believe in God (Mortimer Adler, for example). However, the vast majority of secular humanists do not believe in God or at least do not think it essential to do so.

Among this majority there is a marked division between nonreligious and religious humanists. The division between these two groups is clearly evident when we compare Marxism, which is traditionally nonreligious (atheistic), with our general conception of Western humanism, many forms of which are religious. However, there is also a marked differentiation in the Western world between religious and nonreligious humanism. This difference can be seen when one compares "Humanist Manifesto I" with the subsequent "Secular Humanist Declaration." The framers of the first manifesto called themselves religious humanists and insisted that "to establish such a religion is a major necessity of the present." By contrast, the authors of the declaration eliminate the label *religious humanists* and adopt an antireligious stance. They call themselves "democratic *secular humanists*" who embrace "religious skepticism." Although they acknowledge—somewhat grudgingly—the accomplishment of some good (such as hospitals) by religious people, these secular humanists strongly resent "any efforts by ecclesiastical . . . institutions to shackle free thought."

In short, contemporary secular humanists view religion somewhat inconsistently; some consider religion essential to humanity, while others view it as harmful. Some call secular humanism a religion, whereas others repudiate the term. Some secular humanists encourage religious experience, while others discourage it.

Now it is obvious to any logical mind that these opposite stances cannot both be held. Religion is either essential or harmful to man; it is to be either encouraged or discouraged. One cannot espouse both positions. There are, then, within humanism taken in its broadest sense many contradictory views with regard to religion.

Egocentric versus Social Humanism

All forms of humanism are centered in man. Most are concerned with the welfare of mankind in general; however, the brand of humanism Ayn Rand promotes is focused on the individual. Hers is an egocentric humanism, whereas the other forms generally repudiate egocentricity.

Erich Fromm, for example, speaks of "man for himself"; he does not mean each man for his own personal welfare, however, but each man for *every man.*[1] Fromm calls us to practice an unselfish love that makes mankind its object. By contrast Ayn Rand believes that

---

1. See Erich Fromm, *Man for Himself* (New York: Premier, 1968).

egoistic self-love is our highest and only moral responsibility. We love others only if they serve our self-interest.

It is obvious that both of these forms of humanism cannot be held: if one is affirmed, then the other, as its opposite, must be denied. Even though both Fromm and Rand profess to make man the object of their devotion, their concepts of "man" are so radically different that one view is the antithesis of the other. Again the humanist camp is divided.

Note too that this division is not trivial. Humanists are inconsistent in defining their most fundamental concept, the object of their ultimate commitment. This division is equivalent to the difference between the Christian and the Hindu concept of God. Even though these religions share the term *God*, they are certainly not referring to the same being. Likewise, even though both social and egocentric humanists focus on "man," they are not referring to the same thing.

Existential versus Scientific Humanism

Another serious division in the humanist camp is that between the existential and the scientific (rational) humanists. The scientific humanists, such as Julian Huxley and Carl Sagan,[2] look to the scientific method for man's salvation. On the contrary, the existential humanists, such as Jean-Paul Sartre and Albert Camus, do not find salvation in the objectivity of science but in the subjectivity of man.

Scientific humanists such as B. F. Skinner look to the objective behavioral sciences as the means for changing mankind. Skinner believes that man can be improved if we set aside such notions as freedom and dignity and learn to control his behavior. The existential humanists, on the other hand, see freedom as the very essence of man, and strongly oppose Skinner's behavioral determinism.

Scientific humanists claim that the meaning of man is to be found through objective exploration. The existentialists, on the other hand, regard the objective facts about man to be of little consequence and stress instead an understanding of human subjectivity. Scientific humanism is often materialistic, analyzing man in terms of chemical, physical, and social processes. Existential humanism, on the other hand, stresses the individual, personal, and intangible aspects of man. Scientific humanists say man is completely determined from

2. See Carl Sagan, *Cosmos* (New York: Random House, 1980).

the outside, while existentialists say just the opposite, namely, that man is completely free, that he is determined by what is inside him.

Obviously these two forms of humanism are diametrically opposed. Both cannot be correct, for these philosophies posit two radically different views of humanity and two radically different ways of how we might go about changing man. Again we see conflicting forces within the humanist cause.

Other Internal Opposition

Actually there are many other inconsistencies within the humanist cause; they are probably as great as the differences between the world's basic religions, which most secular humanists oppose. Some secular humanists (for instance, Rand) are capitalists; others (e.g., Karl Marx) are Marxists. Many are for one world government; others oppose it. Some humanists (e.g., Sigmund Freud) believe man is subconsciously determined,[3] others (e.g., Skinner) believe man is socially determined, and still others (e.g., Sartre) believe man is self-determined or free.

In the realm of ethics, although some humanists are willing to admit absolutes or their equivalent in practice, most believe there are no absolutes. Thus it is not surprising that humanists can often be found on both sides of specific ethical issues. Some are for sexual freedom for young people, others are not. Many humanists favor abortion on demand, but some oppose it.[4] Plainly, then, there is no ethical unanimity in the humanistic cause. Instead we find internal conflict on almost every level.

Inconsistencies Within Secular Humanistic Creeds

It may seem to some that the foregoing analysis is unfair. After all, various religions differ too. Why should the pot call the kettle black? This point has legitimacy and reminds us that neither religion nor humanism is really a generic term. The word *humanism*, for example,

3. Freud's humanism is clearly revealed in his *Future of an Illusion* (New York: Doubleday, 1957).

4. For a humanistic attack on abortion on demand see *Aborting America* by Bernard N. Nathanson and Richard L. Ostling (New York: Doubleday, 1979).

does not denote an "essence" or specify an intrinsic set of ideas.[5] Rather, it is a label for a number of points of view that overlap in certain respects.

There is another way of applying the test of consistency to secular humanism, a way that avoids the foregoing problem. It is to examine the common or core beliefs of all secular humanists. These core beliefs include (1) nontheism, (2) naturalism, (3) evolution, (4) ethical relativism, and (5) man's self-sufficiency.

Inconsistency in Nontheism and Naturalism

Two premises common to all forms of secular humanism are nontheism and naturalism. These can be treated together, since if there is no supernatural being (Creator) beyond the universe, then obviously nature is all there is.[6] Often naturalism means that everything can be explained in terms of chemical and physical processes. At a minimum it means that every event in the universe can be explained in terms of the whole universe (the whole system). There is no need to appeal to anything (or anyone) outside the universe to explain any event in the universe or the whole universe itself.

But the very scientific humanists who insist that *everything* can be explained in terms of physical and chemical processes cannot explain their own scientific theories or laws in those terms! For a theory or law about physical processes is obviously not itself a physical process. It is a nonphysical *theory* about physical things. I shall never forget my surprise when confronting an atheistic physics professor with this dilemma. I asked, "What do you mean by the concept of law if everything is to be understood in physical terms?" His amazing response was, *"It is magic!"* He was not joking. And he defended his assertion by noting that the origin of science is magic. It is revealing to note that a purely materialistic world-view must resort to nonmaterial "magic" in order to explain its materialism.

C. S. Lewis made an attempt to show the inconsistency of pure naturalism. Quoting J. B. S. Haldane, Lewis wrote, "If my mental processes are determined wholly by the motion of atoms in my brain,

5. Many modern philosophers of religion have given up on finding an "essence" of religion, and seek rather to describe its experiences and/or practices.

6. See C. S. Lewis, *Miracles* (New York: Macmillan, 1960), p. 12, and our discussion of Lewis's critique in chap. 8.

I have no reason to suppose that my beliefs are true ... and hence I have no reason for supposing my brain to be composed of atoms."[7] That is to say, if naturalism is claiming to be true, then there must be more than mere natural processes; there must be "reason," which is not a purely physical process.

Another way to demonstrate the inconsistency of the naturalism espoused by secular humanism is to show that a basic premise of science which even naturalists hold is contrary to their conclusion that every event in the universe can be explained in terms of the whole universe. This premise, that every event has a cause, is at the basis of scientific research. For scientists are trying to find the explanation for or cause of all events. Now if *every* event has a cause, it follows that the whole universe has a cause. For the universe as conceived by modern science is the sum total of all events at a given time, and the sum total of all caused events needs a cause to explain it.[8]

It will not suffice for the naturalist to say there is something "more" to the universe than the sum of all the events or "parts," for then he is not really explaining everything in terms of the physical parts but in terms of something beyond them. Naturalism is not able to explain either itself or the universe on a purely naturalistic basis.[9]

Inconsistency of Scientific Views

Secular humanists pride themselves on their scientific outlook. They claim to base their beliefs on scientific principles and evidence. At the same time they believe in the theory of evolution. But there are some serious inconsistencies in holding to both of these commitments.

First of all, present scientific evidence, as even many naturalistic and agnostic scientists admit, suggests that the universe began with a Big Bang several billions of years ago.[10] For the second law of thermodynamics says that the universe is running down (that is, the

7. Lewis, *Miracles*, p. 15.

8. For a further discussion of this cosmological argument see my *Christian Apologetics* (Grand Rapids: Baker, 1978), chap. 13.

9. A more systematic critique of naturalism can be found in my *Miracles and Modern Thought* (Grand Rapids: Zondervan, 1982).

10. See the excellent discussion of the Big-Bang theory by the agnostic astronomer Robert Jastrow in his *God and the Astronomers* (New York: W. W. Norton, 1978).

amount of usable energy in the universe is decreasing). If this is so then the universe must have had a beginning, for otherwise it would have run down by now. Furthermore, if the universe came into being billions of years ago, as many scientists believe, then it must have had a cause which brought it into existence. For every event has a cause. This is precisely what the naturalists refuse to accept, namely, a cause (God) who created the whole universe. And yet the scientific principles and evidence they allegedly accept demand that they acknowledge this.

Second, Francesco Redi, Louis Pasteur, and others firmly established the scientific principle that spontaneous generation does not occur. That is, the nonliving never produces the living. The humanistic theory of origin is directly contrary to this dictum of science. For the naturalistic explanation of first life asserts that life arose spontaneously from nonliving chemicals. Yet no scientist has ever *observed* nonliving chemicals spontaneously produce a living organism. Scientists pride themselves that their method is based on observation. But this crucial link in the naturalistic process (nonliving to living) is without any scientific evidence.

But what if scientists succeed in creating life? Will not this then prove naturalistic evolution? First of all, scientists have not yet produced any living organisms from purely nonliving chemicals. They have produced some of the building blocks of life (such as amino acids) from nonliving chemicals. And they have produced different organisms by borrowing the life codes (DNA) of living organisms and splicing genes. But they have not created life from scratch. And even if they could, that would not prove naturalistic evolution. It would prove only that it takes outside intelligent intervention into the natural world to make the living from the nonliving. For *the role of the experimenter is crucial* in producing even amino acids. The chemicals used, for example, must be on the order of a million times more concentrated than they appear naturally anywhere on earth. But intelligent intervention is precisely what the naturalists reject in the creationist view of life. They refuse to admit that it takes intelligence (not mere natural laws) to create life. The missing ingredient in purely naturalistic explanations of the origin of life is intelligence. Force combined with the right chemical elements, time, and chance never produces a complex living product.

We find inconsistency not only in the naturalistic explanation of first life, but also in the explanation of the origin of new life forms.[11] In both the fossil record and the modern world there are many different kinds of life. Yet there is no evidence either in the rocks or in nature that one of these forms of life ever changed (or changes) into an entirely different form of life with new, functioning organs.[12] The *theory* of evolution, which postulates that such changes do occur, is contrary to fundamental principles of science. For nonrational random forces of nature are not adequate to produce highly organized, complex systems such as even the simplest form of life, to say nothing of higher life forms.

Inconsistency in Ethics

The secular humanists of the manifestos claim to be ethical relativists. They claim all values are subject to change. There are no absolutes; all is situational.

However, there is a basic inconsistency in their claims at this point. First of all, is the claim "everything is relative" relative or nonrelative? If it is not relative, then it is an absolute. But then the claim is self-defeating. For it would be an absolute to claim that there are no absolutes. If, on the other hand, the claim "everything is relative" is itself only a relative claim, then we need to ask, "relative to what?" Is it simply based on something that is based on something that is based on something, and so on infinitely?[13] If so, then there is no basis for it. For every "basis" turns out to be based on another. The only way out of this infinite regress is to admit that there is a basis which has no further basis. But this would be to admit an absolute, which the secular humanist denies.

Now let us look at the secular humanists' ethical inconsistency in a practical way. Are they conditionally or unconditionally committed to the premise that some form of secular humanism is true? They

11. See Duane Gish, *Evolution? The Fossils Say No!* (San Diego: Creation-Life, 1972).

12. Ibid., p. 19.

13. C. S. Lewis critiques the infinite regress in *The Abolition of Man* (New York: Macmillan, 1947): "But you cannot go on 'explaining away' for ever: you will find that you have explained explanation itself away. You cannot go on 'seeing through' things for ever. If you see through everything, then everything is transparent. But a wholly transparent world is an invisible world. To 'see through' all things is the same as not to see" (p. 9).

certainly *act* and even *write* as though they were unconditionally committed to it.[14] For in view of new evidence they seem always to revise but never to reject humanism. Their faith seems unshakable. Hence one would conclude their commitment is unconditional. For example, one can scarcely conceive of a situation wherein a secular humanist would *ever* advocate abolition of such basic human values as intellectual freedom or the right to think as one wishes. Likewise, what humanist approves of Hitler's attempt to annihilate all Jews? Now if the humanist never gives up basic human values, then he shows that in practice he believes in them unconditionally or absolutely. This absolutistic belief is inconsistent with his denial of *all* absolutes. Surely no open-minded secular humanist would want to assert that "all values are relative *except* the values of secular humanism." This would be a radical and dogmatic case of special pleading—an attitude humanists deplore in others. Thus no matter which way they turn secular humanists manifest a basic inconsistency in ethics.

Inconsistency Regarding Education

Secular humanists are dedicated to education. They consider it a must for mankind. Indeed, education is their means of salvation. But their view of education conflicts with some of their other central tenets. Consider the following three beliefs, all of which were firmly espoused by the authors of "Humanist Manifestos I and II": (1) no religion should be given a preferred position by the state; (2) humanism is a religion; and (3) everyone should receive a state-supported education in basic humanistic values. Such an education would be an education in the values of the religion of secular humanism. This would give a privileged position to one religion, that of secular

14. William Kingdon Clifford wrote that he could not possibly tamper with the "truth" of his humanistic beliefs, even though it would have been comforting to change them (and believe in immortality) when he was bereaved of his son. In response Elton Trueblood said, "Why should men like Clifford and Huxley be so finicky about the 'truth' if there is nothing in the world but matter and our feeble lives? Their carefulness becomes fully rational, however, *if there is One to whom their dishonesty becomes disloyalty.* The practice of the honest atheist frequently denies the conscious import of his words, because he is acting in a way which makes no sense *unless his conscious conclusions are untrue*" (*Philosophy of Religion* [New York: Harper & Row, 1957], p. 115).

humanism, thus violating the separation of church and state. Perhaps this inconsistency is what forced the authors of the "Secular Humanist Declaration" to omit the claim that humanism is a religion. Nonetheless, secular humanism is a religion both legally and actually; therefore it should not have a privileged position in public schools.

Another inconsistency regarding education is manifest in the "Secular Humanist Declaration." "The first principle of democratic secular humanism," the authors say, "is its commitment to free inquiry." They continue, "We oppose any tyranny over the mind of man. . . . Free inquiry requires that we tolerate diversity of opinion and that we respect the rights of individuals to express their beliefs, however unpopular they may be." But despite this fine statement of ideals, just two pages later the same declaration rejects the teaching of scientific creationism in the classroom on the grounds that scientific creationism "is a serious threat both to academic freedom and to the integrity of the educational process."[15] It would be hard to find a clearer example of a violation of the humanists' own principle of academic freedom. For them "freedom" in the classroom apparently means only the freedom to teach their own points of view.

It is a tragic truth that secular humanists are open-minded about anything that is in accord with their humanistic commitments and firmly closed-minded to anything else. This is manifest when one contrasts the secular humanists' stances at two famous creation-evolution trials. At the Scopes trial of 1925 the secular humanists' lawyer, Clarence Darrow, argued that it is "bigotry for public schools to teach only one theory of origins."[16] Fifty-six years later, at the "Scopes II" trial in Arkansas (which was to decide whether creation could be taught along with evolution), the secular humanists argued in effect (and won!) that it is bigotry to teach two theories of origin![17] Apparently what secular humanists mean is that it is bigotry to teach only one view when creation is that view, but not when evolution is that view! Such is the glaring inconsistency of secular humanism's educational approach.

15. "A Secular Humanist Declaration," in *Free Inquiry*, Winter 1980 – 81, pp. 4, 6.

16. See R. O'Bannon, *Creation, Evolution and Public Education* 5, Symposium on Tennessee's evolution laws, May 18, 1974.

17. For a documentary, eyewitness account of the "Scopes II" trial, see *The Creator in the Courtroom*, by N. L. Geisler, Al Brooke, and Mark Keough (Milford, Mich.: Mott Media, 1982).

There is no completely unified humanistic movement. Actually what is called humanism is a broad range of views often contradictory to each other in many respects. Some humanists are in favor of religion and others are opposed to it. Some are communists and others are capitalists. Some are egoists and some are philanthropists. However, the various kinds of humanism agree on a few central beliefs. These have been crystallized in two manifestos and a declaration. When these basic common beliefs of secular humanism are examined carefully, they reveal certain internal inconsistencies. Although they claim to be humane, they promote the killing of innocent life (abortion, euthanasia). Although they claim to be scientific, they violate basic laws of science. Although they claim to be rational, they violate fundamental principles of reason. Although they claim that all ethics is relative, they do so with an absolute statement. In the final analysis, then, secular humanism is not a consistent position.

13

The Religious Inadequacies of Secular Humanism

Secular Humanism as a Religion

Before we can discuss the inadequacies of secular humanism as a religion, it should be pointed out that secular humanism is indeed a religion. Secular humanists often claim to be deeply religious and to have religious experiences. Julian Huxley, for example, frankly admitted that he had had deeply religious experiences:

> On Easter Sunday, early in the morning, I got up at daybreak, before anyone else was about, let myself out, ran across to a favourite copse, penetrated to where I knew the wild cherry grew, and there, in the spring dew, picked a great armful of the lovely stuff, which I brought back, with a sense of its being an acceptable offering, to the house. Three or four Easters running I remember doing this. I was fond of solitude and of nature, and had a passion for wild flowers: but this was only a general basis.... But when sanctity is in the air, as at Easter, then it can have free play.[1]

Friedrich Schleiermacher defined religion as a feeling of absolute dependence on the All.[2] Sigmund Freud admitted to having had

1. Julian Huxley, *Religion Without Revelation* (New York: Mentor, 1957), p. 70.
2. Schleiermacher, *On Religion: Speeches to Its Cultural Despisers*, trans. J. Onian (New York: Frederick Ungar, 1955), p. 39.

such a feeling himself, though he did not call it religious. Paul Tillich defined religion as an ultimate commitment.[3] In this sense of the word *religion* most secular humanists have a religious commitment to humanity. The authors of "Humanist Manifesto II" say that "commitment to all humankind is the highest commitment of which we are capable"[4]—to borrow Tillich's phrase, an "ultimate commitment."[5] John Dewey defined the religious as any ideal pursued with great conviction because of its general and enduring value. In this sense humanism certainly involves a religious experience.

Erich Fromm was even willing to use the word *God* of the "ultimate commitment to all of mankind." And although he wished to dissociate himself from what he called "authoritarian" beliefs, he did admit that his humanstic beliefs were religious. He felt that his devotion to mankind as a whole was a religious devotion, and the object of that devotion he called God.[6] Although the Jewish existentialist, Martin Buber, regarded the word *God* as the most heavily laden in our vocabulary, he insisted that by loving other persons one has fulfilled his religious obligation to "God."[7]

Even the atheistic humanists, who deny that there is any validity to religious experience, often admit that they once had such experiences. Jean-Paul Sartre told of such experiences as a child: "I believed. In my nightshirt, kneeling on the bed, with my hands together, I said my prayers every day, but I thought of God less and less often."[8] Likewise Bertrand Russell admitted to once believing in God, as did Friedrich Nietzsche and others.

It is obvious from these examples that whether in the past or present, whether in the form of devotion to God, to the All, or to mankind, many humanists admit having had an experience which could be classified religious. And although "Humanist Manifesto I"

3. Tillich, *Ultimate Concern*, ed. D. Mackenzie Brown (London: SCM, 1965), pp. 7 – 8, 30.

4. "Humanist Manifesto II," in *Humanist Manifestos I & II*, ed. Paul Kurtz (Buffalo: Prometheus, 1973), p. 23.

5. See John Whitehead, "The Establishment of the Religion of Secular Humanism and Its First Amendment Implications," in *Texas Tech Law Review* 10, no. 1 (1978): 14.

6. See Fromm, *Psychoanalysis and Religion* (New Haven: Yale University, 1967), pp. 49, 54, 87.

7. See Buber, *I and Thou*, in *The Writings of Martin Buber*, ed. Will Herberg (New York: Meridian Books, 1968), p. 55.

8. Sartre, *Words* (New York: George Braziller, 1964), p. 102.

calls for giving up belief in any form of extraterrestrial being,[9] many atheistic humanists do insist that they have not thereby forsaken religion. In fact, the religious urge was so great in one eminent humanist (Auguste Comte) that he set up a humanist sect and installed himself as the high priest! One point emerges clearly: in the sense in which the word *religious* is currently defined by dictionaries, philosophers, and theologians (including humanists themselves), humanism is a religion.

Not only do many humanists claim to be religious, but the United States courts have come to recognize secular humanism as a religion. The decision in the case of the *United States v. Kauten* (1943) allowed conscientious objectors exemption from the military draft even if they did not believe in a deity. The circuit court which heard this case stated, "[Conscientious objection] may justly be regarded as a response of the individual to an inward mentor, call it conscience or God, that is for many persons at the present time the equivalent of what has always been thought a religious impulse."[10]

The following year (1944) the same court ruled in the case of the *United States v. Ballard* that "[freedom of religion] embraces the right to maintain theories of life and death and of the hereafter which are rank heresy to followers of the orthodox faiths."[11] In 1961 in the case of *Torcaso v. Watkins* the United States Supreme Court unanimously held that it was unconstitutional for Maryland to require belief in God as a condition for becoming a notary public. The justices were specific in identifying secular humanism as a religion: "Among religions in this country which do not teach what would generally be considered a belief in the existence of God are Buddhism, Taoism, Ethical Culture, Secular Humanism and others."[12]

In 1965 the Supreme Court ruled in the case of the *United States v. Seeger* that any belief can be classified as religious if it is "sincere and meaningful [and if it] occupies a place in the life of its possessor parallel to that filled by the orthodox belief in God."[13] Having consulted the theologian Paul Tillich, the Court defined religion as "[belief] based upon a power or being or upon a faith, to which all else is

9. See "Humanist Manifesto I," ed. Kurtz, pp. 14 – 16.
10. Whitehead, "Establishment," p. 10.
11. Ibid., p. 11.
12. Ibid., p. 13.
13. Ibid., p. 14.

subordinate or upon which all else is ultimately dependent."[14] Thus religion is practiced by atheists, agnostics, and secular humanists as well as adherents of "orthodox" faiths.

One of the implications of granting secular humanism full religious status is that it too is now susceptible to the First Amendment's prohibition of the establishment of religion. In the case of the *School District of Abington Township, Pa., v. Schempp* (1963), Justice Tom Clark ruled that "the State may not establish a 'religion of secularism' ... thus preferring those who believe in no religion over those who do believe."[15] The same prohibition is repeated in other decisions. Thus the Court has officially recognized secular humanism as a religion.

There are many other indications secular humanism is a religion. There is a journal called *Religious Humanism*. The Unitarian Universalist Association (resulting from a merger of the Unitarian Association and the Universalist Church) is humanistic in its beliefs. Huxley called his philosophy "the religion of evolutionary humanism." More recently the secular humanist Konstantin Kolenda has written a book entitled *Religion Without God* (1976).

Although some secular humanists avoid the term *religion*,[16] they cannot avoid the fact that others with the *same* basic beliefs classify those beliefs as a religion and that the United States Supreme Court has specifically recognized secular humanism as a religion. Indeed, secular humanism meets all the requirements of the current popular and legal definitions of "religion."

The Inadequacies of Secular Humanism as a Religion

Psychological Inadequacy

In a very revealing article in *Humanist Magazine* (1964) a secular humanist points out several ways in which secular humanism is psychologically inadequate as a religion. The article is entitled "What's Wrong with Humanism?" In it the indictment is made that the move-

14. Ibid.
15. Ibid., p. 18.
16. See Paul Beattie, "Humanism: Secular or Religious," in *Free Inquiry*, Winter 1980 — 81, pp. 11 — 15.

ment is too intellectual and almost "clinically detached from life." In order to resolve this problem and to reach the masses with the humanist message, the suggestion is made to develop a humanist Bible, a humanist hymnal, Ten Commandments for humanists, and even confessional practices (testimonies)! In addition, "the use of hypnotic techniques—music and other psychological devices—during humanist services would give the audience that deep spiritual experience and they would emerge refreshed and inspired with their humanist faith."[17] Rarely do humanists speak so freely about the psychological inadequacies of their system and the need to borrow Christian practices to rectify them.

T. M. Kitwood has summarized the deficiencies of secular humanism well. He charges that "humanism does not evoke a response from the whole person, intellect, will and emotion." Further, humanists "lack originality when making positive statements about man's life, and easily descend to the platitudinous."[18] Another weakness of secular humanism is its failure to reckon realistically with the facts of human nature. Some humanists have manifested an incredible naiveté about life. For example, John Stuart Mill wrote that his father "felt as if all would be gained if the whole population were taught to read."[19] Even Bertrand Russell thought that "if we could learn to love our neighbor the world would quickly become a paradise for us all."[20] Finally, Kitwood charges humanists with being "an aristocratic body, and as such insulated from some of the more terrible realities of life."[21] One conclusion emerges clearly: secular humanism does not meet the psychological demands made of religion.

Social Inadequacy

Secular humanism often has noble social goals, but in general it lacks sufficient motivating power to accomplish them. As William James pointed out in his classic treatment of religious experience, the men who set this world afire are themselves set aflame by another world. Such men, not the secularists, are the saints. They believe in

17. "What's Wrong With Humanism?" in *Humanist Magazine* (1964), quoted in T. M. Kitwood, *What Is Human?* (Downers Grove, Ill.: Inter-Varsity, 1970), p. 49.
18. Kitwood, *What Is Human?*, p. 48.
19. Ibid., p. 50.
20. Ibid.
21. Ibid., p. 51.

a supernatural world, which secular humanism denies. In James's own words,

> In a general way, then and "on the whole," . . . our testing of religion by practical common sense and the empirical method, leave[s] it in possession of its towering place in history. . . . Let us be saints, then, if we can, whether or not we succeed visibly and temporally.[22]

Spiritual Inadequacy

Although secular humanists often confess to having religious, even mystical, experiences, they deny these involve a personal God. But these experiences are strangely personal for having no personal object. Those who have them speak of "loyalty," "devotion," and "love"—but directed to what? These are terms that make sense only when they have a personal object. Who, for example, can fall in love with the Pythagorean theorem? Or who would be religiously moved by the exhortation, "Prepare to meet thy $E=MC^2$"? As Elton Trueblood insightfully observed, "The joy and wonder which men feel in the search for truth, including the quality of feeling of those scientists who think of themselves as materialists . . . is the *same kind of feeling we know best when there is real communication between two finite minds.*"[23]

There can be no true devotion without a personal object. Perhaps this is what accounts for the lack of a truly satisfying spiritual experience among humanists. For example, Huxley frankly admitted that his religious experience became dimmer over the years. He wrote, "I had been used, ever since the age of fifteen or sixteen, to having such moments come to me naturally. . . . But now . . . they were vouchsafed in diminishing measure, and (although sometimes with great intensity) more fleetingly."[24] Sartre confessed that his religious experience ceased when he dismissed God from his life: "I had all the more difficulty of getting rid of Him in that He had installed Himself at the back of my head. . . . I collared the Holy Ghost in the cellar and threw Him out. . . . Atheism is a cruel and long-range affair; I think I've carried it through."[25] Sartre's confession of the difficulty

22. James, *Varieties of Religious Experiences* (New York: Mentor, 1958), p. 290.
23. Trueblood, *Philosophy of Religion* (New York: Harper & Row, 1957), p. 115.
24. Huxley, *Religion Without Revelation*, p. 77.
25. Sartre, *Words*, pp. 252 – 253.

and even cruelty of life without God should not be surprising to anyone who truly understands the human personality. For humans find greatest satisfaction in the personal. They are fulfilled in what Buber called an "I-Thou" experience, not an "I-it" experience. That is, persons are satisfied best by other persons (subjects), not by things (objects). Hence it is not strange that a religious experience is not going to be fully satisfying unless it involves a personal object.

Philosophical Inadequacy

Paul Tillich described a religious experience as an ultimate commitment, but he also recognized that not every ultimate commitment is made to something that is itself ultimate. He believed that to be ultimately committed to what is less than ultimate is really idolatry.[26] Martin Buber pointed out that idols can be mental as well as metal.[27] Combining these two insights, we may note that when humanists make some finite ideal or goal the object of their religious commitment, they are really idolaters.

Mankind is not infinite or ultimate. By their own confession humanists recognize human life to be mortal. Even the race itself may someday be annihilated or become extinct. Why then do secular humanists treat mankind as if it were eternal? Why an unswerving commitment to that which is changing and even perishing? Why such a purposeful devotion to what is the product of a blind evolutionary process? And why make something so big out of the tiny human microbe on a speck of cosmic dust in a minute corner of an unimaginably vast universe? Is it not the height of humanistic arrogance for man to endow himself with divinity?[28] The infinite devotion that humanists give to man is due only to the Infinite, not to the finite. In short, unless the object of one's ultimate commitment is truly ultimate, it is religiously and philosophically inadequate. An ultimate concern should be reserved only for an object worthy of it. The only thing actually worthy of an ultimate commitment is actually ultimate. Finite man is not ultimate, and such unreserved devotion as secular humanists give to man should be given only to an infinite, personal God.

26. See Tillich, *Ultimate Concern*, p. 57.
27. Buber. *Eclipse of God* (New York: Harper & Row, 1952), p. 62.
28. See chap. 15.

The Need for God

One of the strongest indications that men need God is found in the experiences of the very men who deny the need for God. The confessions of numerous secular humanists are ample testimony to this point. A brief survey of the writings of secular humanists (some of whom acknowledge a religious experience, some of whom do not) will underscore the truth of Augustine's famous dictum that the heart is restless until it finds its rest in God.

Friedrich Nietzsche, who postulated that there is no eternal God, but rather an eternal recurrence of the same events, bemoaned his intolerable loneliness as compared to other poets and philosophers who believed in God:

> I hold up before myself the images of Dante and Spinoza, who were better at accepting the lot of solitude ... and in the end ... all those who somehow still had a "God" for company. ... My life now consists in the wish that it might be otherwise ... and that somebody might make *my* "truths" appear incredible to me.[29]

The contemporary atheist Jean-Paul Sartre admitted, "I needed God."[30] Furthermore, "I reached out for religion, I longed for it, it was the remedy. Had it been denied me, I would have invented it myself."[31] And the French atheist Albert Camus asserted, "Nothing can discourage the appetite for divinity in the heart of man."[32] His ironic confession that the church must be built even though there is no God reminds one of the dictum that those who deny God with the top of their minds nevertheless cannot avoid Him in the bottom of their hearts.

Sigmund Freud claimed that the concept of God is not based in reality, yet he admitted that he too had the Schleiermachean sense of absolute dependence. Freud himself experienced "a sense of man's insignificance and impotence in the face of the universe."[33] He acknowledged that this sense of absolute dependence is inescapable

---

29. Nietzsche, *The Portable Nietzsche*, ed. and trans. Walter Kaufmann (Princeton, N.J.: Princeton University, 1968), p. 441.

30. Sartre, *Words*, p. 102.

31. Ibid., p. 97.

32. Camus, *The Rebel* (New York: Alfred Knopf, 1956), p. 147.

33. Freud, *The Future of an Illusion* (New York: Doubleday, 1957), p. 57.

and cannot be overcome by science. The same divine need can be sensed in Samuel Beckett's *Waiting for Godot*, the title of which is reminiscent of Martin Heidegger's phrase, "waiting for God." Likewise, Franz Kafka's novels express lonely man's persistent attempts to find some meaningful cosmic otherness. Walter Kaufmann goes so far as to confess that "religion is rooted in man's aspiration to transcend himself. . . . Whether he worships idols or strives to perfect himself, man is the God-intoxicated ape."[34]

Other nonbelievers, such as Julian Huxley, have seen great benefits arising from man's apparently incurable religious needs. Huxley spoke of "the possibility of enjoying experiences of transcendent rapture, physical or mystical, aesthetic or religious, . . . of attaining inner harmony and peace, which puts a man above the cares and worries of daily life."[35] What is this but another description of what the religious man calls "God"? What is more, Huxley spoke of life as being "intolerable" without such religious experiences.[36]

If the need for God is seemingly so irradicable, even in humanists, then why is it that many thousands of men think they are capable of living without God? There are several possible answers to this important question. It has been suggested that the unbeliever is inconsistent at this point. Jackson Pollock, for example, believed the universe is random and without design. Yet he wisely decided not to proceed in a random manner when it came to his hobby of mushrooms. For he realized that there is a pattern as to which ones are poisonous and which are not. Thus his life was inconsistent with his philosophy.

In a frank interview with the *Chicago Sun-Times*, the famous atheist Will Durant admitted that the common man will fall to pieces morally if he thinks there is no God. "On the other hand," said Durant, "a man like me . . . I survive morally because I retain the moral code that was taught me along with the religion, while I have discarded the religion, which was Roman Catholicism." Durant continued,

> You and I are living on a shadow . . . because we are operating on the Christian ethical code which was given us, unfused with the Christian faith. . . . But what will happen to our children . . . ? We are not giving

34. Kaufmann, *Critique of Religion and Philosophy* (New York: Doubleday, 1965), pp. 354 – 355, 399.
35. Quoted by Kitwood in *What Is Human?*, p. 38.
36. See Huxley, *Religion Without Revelation*, p. 77.

them an ethics warmed up with a religious faith. They are living on the shadow of a shadow.[37]

Indeed it is difficult to live on a shadow, and more so on a shadow's shadow! But this is precisely how humanists are living when they try to live without God.

Often ethics or aesthetics becomes an atheist's surrogate for God, but this will be satisfying only insofar as it rides piggyback on some belief in God. As Martin Marty noted, atheism occurs and can occur only where belief is or has been. This "explains why atheism ... is itself a proof, by reason of its invariably polemical character (witness Lucretius in antiquity, or Nietzsche and Marx in the modern world), of the reality and depth of the religious impulse."[38] When a man tries to overthrow everything—even the aesthetic and ethical shadows—he finds, to use Sartre's words, that "atheism is a cruel and long-range affair." Camus echoed this sentiment: "For anyone who is alone, without God and without a master, the weight of days is dreadful."[39]

Sartre found atheism "cruel," Camus found it "dreadful," Huxley "intolerable," and Nietzsche literally maddening. In short, even atheists evidence the need for God. Some of them try to live totally without God; they tend to commit suicide or go insane. Others are inconsistent: they live on the ethical or aesthetic shadow of Christian truth while they deny the reality that made the shadow. But whatever the case, all men—including unbelievers—evidence a definite need for God. Viktor Frankl, in a recent book entitled *The Unconscious God*, contends that "man has always stood in an intentional relation to transcendence, even if only on an unconscious level." In this sense, he says, all men seek the "Unconscious God."[40]

While secular humanists claim that their beliefs constitute a religion, they deny the need for a personal God. But the evidence of their own experience does not support their claim. For the "religious" experience they have is not psychologically, socially, spiritually, or philosophically adequate. Psychologically, their "ideal" lacks personal

37. *Chicago Sun-Times*, 24 August 1975, Section 1 B, p. 8.

38. Marty, *Varieties of Unbelief* (New York: Doubleday, 1966), pp. 119 – 120.

39. Camus, *The Fall* (New York: Random House, 1956), p. 133.

40. Frankl, *The Unconscious God*, quoted in a review, "The Roots of Commitment," by Michael Macdonald, in *Christianity Today*, 19 November 1976, p. 43.

appeal; socially, it lacks motivating power. Spiritually, it does not offer a *personal* object of devotion, for which even the atheistic humanists have betrayed a deep need. And philosophically, it does not offer an ultimate value worthy of ultimate personal commitment.

According to the existentialist Jean-Paul Sartre, man needs God but there is no God; such is the absurdity of life. But to say this is both irrational and cruel. It is irrational because it assumes that there is no reason in the universe, that the universe is mocking us, and that man's most basic need is forever unfulfillable. It is like saying all men are dying of thirst and there is no water anywhere, or that men are starving to death and there is no food anywhere! Now while it is true that some desert wanderers never find an oasis, it is not rational to therefore assume that there are no oases anywhere. Likewise, while it is true that some men never find God, it is not rational therefore to assume that He does not exist. Certainly humanists, who pride themselves on their rationality, should be among the last people to assume the universe is ultimately irrational. Indeed, they often claim human reason is our primary means of salvation.

Freud was right when he labeled a mere *wish* an illusion.[41] But the experience of both believer and unbeliever is that God is more than a mere desire; He is a *need* of every heart. And it is cruel to deny men their basic needs.

Is it not cruel to detour a thirsty soul from his search to find the God who can satisfy his longings? This is especially so in view of the fact that there are many pilgrims who, having found the fountain of life, are now stationed along the way to testify to its existence. These include such great minds as Augustine, Aquinas, Pascal, and Kierkegaard. Certainly it is cruelly unjust for someone who has not found God, and therefore claims He does not exist, to tell another to give up his search. As to whether true love can be found in this life, it is better to consult a happily married man than a disappointed bachelor. Furthermore, if men really need God, as even many secular humanists confess, then one is foolish to give up his search before it has begun. Certainly secular humanists have not provided any solid evidence that they have found an ultimately meaningful and enjoyable life without God.

41. Freud, *The Future of an Illusion*, pp. 48 – 50.

14

The Philosophical Insufficiency of Secular Humanism

There are a number of areas wherein the philosophical insufficiencies of secular humanism are manifest. We will briefly describe insufficiencies in the areas of epistemology, metaphysics, and ethics.

Epistemological Insufficiencies

Most secular humanists place strong emphasis on human reason.[1] Indeed, they pride themselves on being rational. However, in the final analysis their system is insufficiently rational. This is evident in three ways: (1) in their failure to carry through the fundamental principles of reason, (2) in their denial of absolute truth, and (3) in their inability to justify their truth claims.

Failure in the Use of Reason

It is a fundamental principle of all rational thought that every event has a reason or cause.[2] If this is the case then the natural

1. See "Humanist Manifesto I," art. 11, and "Humanist Manifesto II," arts. 4, 11, in *Humanist Manifestos I & II*, ed. Paul Kurtz (Buffalo: Prometheus, 1973); and "A Secular Humanist Declaration," in *Free Inquiry* (Winter 1980 – 81), arts. 1, 4, 8.
2. Even the skeptic David Hume wrote (in a letter to John Steward), "I never asserted so absurd a proposition as that anything might arise without a cause" (*The Letters of David Hume*, ed. J. Y. T. Grieg [Oxford: Clarendon, 1932], vol. 1, p. 187).

world must have a cause, since the universe as viewed by modern science is a series of events. Yet secular humanists maintain that the natural world needs no cause beyond itself.[3] But to claim that there is a reason or cause for *every* event, and yet to insist that there is no reason for *all* events (i.e., the whole universe), is inconsistent. For if every page in this book is paper then surely all the pages together are paper. The whole is the sum of all the parts. What is true of the nature of each part is most assuredly true of the whole. Hence if each "part" (event) in the universe has a cause, then surely the whole universe has a cause.

In avoiding this conclusion by claiming that the whole universe does not need a cause, only the parts do, secular humanists are being irrational. They are not carrying reason through to its logical conclusion. For they are saying that one can ask for a reason only for *part* of the events of the universe, but not for *all* the events of the universe.

Such "reasoning" by the secular humanists is particularly strange in the light of their emphasis on modern science. For modern science has shown that the universe is not eternal.[4] One of the most fundamental principles of science is the second law of thermodynamics. This states that in a closed system (such as the universe) the amount of usable energy is decreasing. This being the case, the universe will sooner or later run out of usable energy. Now if the universe can run out of energy then its energy cannot be infinite, since infinite energy cannot run out. And if the energy in the universe is not infinite or eternal, there must have been a beginning. But if the universe had a beginning then reason demands that we ask what caused the universe to begin. A failure to ask this question is to avoid the ultimate rational question. The secular humanists seem to say that it is reasonable to ask the cause of every event in the universe except the first one! In other words there is a cause for *every* event, but there was no cause for the first one. But this is a contradiction in reason. A possible solution might be to say that there is a cause

3. Bertrand Russell said (in a debate with Frederick Copleston), "I see no reason whatsoever to suppose that the total has any cause whatsoever" ("A Debate on the Existence of God," in *The Existence of God*, ed. John Hick [New York: Macmillan, 1964], p. 175).

4. See Robert Jastrow, *God and the Astronomers* (New York: W. W. Norton, 1978), pp. 14 – 29.

for every event *except* the first one. But this is to make an exception to the fundamental principle of reason (every event has a cause) and, thus, to be insufficiently reasonable. Indeed, it is to be *ultimately* irrational, since it denies the need for an ultimate reason. In either event secular humanism is not sufficiently rational.

Denial of Absolute Truth

There is another epistemological problem with secular humanism: the denial of absolute truth. Most secular humanists realize the pitfall of admitting there is absolute truth. Augustine argued that the only adequate basis for an absolute truth would be an absolute Mind[5] (i.e., God). But this secular humanists are not willing to acknowledge. Hence it seems better to most of them to avoid the claim that anything is absolutely true.

However, it is not easy to say that there is no absolute truth. Indeed, it seems to be impossible. For the statement "no truth can be absolute" is itself either absolute or not. If it is absolute, then it is self-destructive of its own claim that there is no absolute truth. If it is not an absolute truth, then it may be wrong. And if it may be wrong then it follows that some truth may be absolute. Thus the humanist claim that there is no absolute truth is either self-defeating or unsuccessful.

Let us make the point another way. An absolute truth would be one which admits of no exceptions. Now the humanist claim that "there are exceptions to every statement" either applies to itself or it does not. If it does apply to itself, then there are exceptions to the statement that "there are exceptions to every statement." This would mean there are some statements without exceptions, that is, absolute truths. On the other hand, if the statement "there are exceptions to every statement" does not apply to itself, then it is a statement without exceptions. In either case, then, one cannot avoid coming face to face with some form of absolute truth (unless of course one does not think or state anything—which secular humanists are not prone to do).

5. See Augustine, *The Free Choice of the Will*, trans. Robert P. Russell, in *The Fathers of the Church* (Washington, D.C.: Catholic University of America, 1968), vol. 59, chaps. 3 – 20.

Inability to Justify Truth Claims

Secular humanists make truth claims. This is why they teach and write books—they claim to know some truths about the universe. The Christian claims Christianity is true. The secular humanist claims secular humanism is true. But both views cannot be true. If one is true then the other view must be false. But how do we decide? Epistemologically we can decide the issue by asking for a *justification* of the truth claim, since unjustified truth claims are not presenting proven *truths* but unproven *beliefs*. One can believe anything, but when he claims to *know* it is true, then he must be prepared to give some justification for his claim to truth.

One of the basic principles in epistemology is that whatever is not self-evident (i.e., known to be true in terms of itself alone) must be known in terms of something else.[6] Neither Christian nor secular-humanist claims to truth are obviously self-evident. Now if neither Christian nor secular-humanist claims about ultimate reality are self-evidently true in terms of themselves, then (if they are indeed true) they must be true in terms of something else. Herein lies the epistemological problem for secular humanism—*every* knowledge claim cannot be justified in terms of another; there must ultimately be something which is not justified in terms of something else. To deny this would be tantamount to saying there is *no* justification. For to say this truth claim about ultimate reality is based on that one, and that one on another, and so on infinitely, is to put off forever the promised basis of justification. Forever avoiding the epistemological "debt" is the same as refusing to pay it altogether!

C. S. Lewis once said, "Reason might conceivably be found to depend on [another reason], and so on; it would not matter how far this process was carried provided you found Reason coming from Reason at each stage. It is only when you are asked to believe in Reason coming from non-reason that you must cry Halt, for if you don't all thought is discredited. It is therefore obvious that sooner or later you must admit a Reason which exists absolutely on its own."[7] In other words, there cannot be an infinite regress of truth claims any more than there can be an infinite regress of causes of events. Not everything can be caused; something must be doing the

6. For an excellent statement of this point see C. S. Lewis, *The Abolition of Man* (New York: Macmillan, 1947), p. 91 (also quoted above in chap. 8, pp. 100 – 101).

7. C. S. Lewis, *Miracles* (New York: Macmillan, 1947), pp. 27 – 28.

causing. Likewise, no claim to knowledge by either the Christian or the secular humanist can be regarded as valid unless there is some *justification* for that claim. Now justification for truth claims about ultimate reality cannot go on forever. Sooner or later we must arrive at some self-justifying or ultimate truth which needs no further explanation. Since truth claims are made by minds, this ultimate truth must rest in some ultimate Mind which needs no further justification because it knows all that is knowable in terms of itself and not in terms of something (or someone) else.

Metaphysical Insufficiencies

The View of Mind

Most secular humanists deny that mind or spirit can survive the dissolution of matter.[8] They are either materialists (denying mind altogether) or some kind of reductionists, claiming that mind is dependent on matter.

The purely materialist view[9] is clearly self-defeating. For surely the materialist *theory* is not made up of matter. That is, the *theory* about matter has no matter in it. The *idea* that all is made of molecules does not itself consist of molecules. For the *thought* about all matter must itself stand over and above matter. If the thought about matter is part of matter then it cannot be a thought about *all* matter, since being a part of matter it cannot transcend itself to make a pronouncement about *all* matter. Mind (or its thoughts) can transcend matter only if it is more than matter. But if it is more than matter then matter is not all that exists.

Some materialists, however, are not so easily refuted. They admit that mind is more than matter but deny that mind can exist inde-

8. J. M. E. McTaggart and C. J. Ducasse are exceptions to the rule. They are openly atheistic and yet believe in the immortality of the soul.

9. Thomas Hobbes once wrote, "The world (I mean not the earth only . . . , but the *universe*, that is, the whole mass of all things that are) is corporeal, that is to say, body; and hath the dimensions of magnitude, namely, length, breadth, and depth: also every part of body is likewise body, and that which is not body is no part of the universe: and because the universe is all, that which is no part of it is nothing, and consequently nowhere" (*Leviathan*, in Great Books of the Western World, ed. Robert Maynard Hutchins [Chicago: Encyclopedia Britannica, 1952], vol. 23, p. 269).

pendently of matter. They insist that mind is more than matter the way the whole is somehow "more" than the sum of its parts. For instance, a whole motor obviously has something more than all its individual parts spread over the floor of a garage. Nonetheless, when the parts are destroyed, the "whole" motor is destroyed too. Likewise, a mind is more than matter but it is dependent on matter and ceases to exist when man's material parts dissolve. So goes the secular humanists' argument.

Although this materialistic argument is less apparently self-defeating than the first one, it is nonetheless equally wrong. For it affirms that mind is ultimately dependent on matter. This statement claims to be a truth about all mind and matter. We have just seen that no statement about *all* matter can be dependent for its truth upon matter. For one cannot stand outside all matter to make an affirmation about all matter and yet simultaneously claim he is really standing inside matter, dependent upon it. Now if, as the premise being considered asserts, mind is completely dependent on matter, then it cannot make statements from a vantage point beyond matter. And if its statements are not from a standpoint independent of matter, then they are not really statements about *all* matter. For one must step beyond something to see it all. The whole cannot be seen from within. Thus mind cannot legitimately make the statement "mind is dependent on matter," for what appears to be transcendent knowledge actually rests on an immanent basis of operation.

The View of Nature

Secular humanists are naturalists.[10] As such they believe nature is all there is. They insist no supernatural cause of the universe exists. This means that nature is uncaused. The material universe is self-sufficient. But this view has very serious problems. For according to modern science, nature consists of a series of events.[11] And the principle of causality declares that every event has a cause. Thus if nature is the sum total of all events then nature as a whole needs a cause.

10. For the modern attack on the supernatural see David Hume, *An Inquiry Concerning Human Understanding*, The Library of Liberal Arts, ed. Charles W. Hendel (New York: Bobbs-Merrill, 1955), vol. 10; and Antony Flew, "Miracles," in *The Encyclopedia of Philosophy*, ed. Paul Edwards (New York; Macmillan, 1967), vol. 5, pp. 346 — 353.

11. See Alfred North Whitehead, *Process and Reality* (New York: Harper & Row, 1929), pp. 13 — 14.

For if each "part" is caused then the whole must be caused too. Adding up effects never equals a cause. The sum total of all dependent things is itself dependent.

Some secular humanists have attempted to avoid this conclusion by postulating that the whole of nature is more than the parts. Hence the parts can be dependent (or caused), they say, but the whole can be independent (or uncaused). But this will not work. If the naturalist postulates that the whole is independent of the parts, then he has admitted what the supernaturalist insists on. For a whole which is uncaused, independent, and more than the sum total of all the parts of the universe is exactly what the supernaturalist identifies with God. An uncaused, independent cause of everything in the universe is metaphysically identical to the supernaturalist's concept of God.[12]

Another way to see this same point is to ask the naturalist, if all the contingent (dependent) parts of the universe were taken away, would there be anything left? That is, would the whole cease to exist if the parts ceased to exist? If with the destruction of the parts the whole were to cease to exist, then it is not uncaused and independent. Rather, it too is dependent and in need of a cause beyond it. On the other hand, if the whole were to continue to exist even if all parts were destroyed, then it truly transcends nature. In this case it would be the supernatural cause on which the existence of everything in the natural world rests. In either case naturalism has proven to be metaphysically insufficient.

Ethical Insufficiency

It is common for secular humanists to deny moral absolutes. "Humanist Manifesto II" reads, "We affirm that moral values derive their source from human experience. Ethics is *autonomous* and *situational,* needing no theological or ideological sanctions."[13] God is ruled out as a source of value or moral law—"humanism asserts that the nature of the universe depicted by modern science makes unacceptable any supernatural or cosmic guarantees of human values."[14]

12. For a more complete critique of naturalism see my *Miracles and Modern Thought* (Grand Rapids: Zondervan, 1982).
13. "Humanist Manifesto II," p. 8.
14. Ibid.

In their efforts to avoid moral absolutes, secular humanists even preface their manifestos with guarded remarks such as, "Those who sign *Humanist Manifesto II* disclaim that they are setting forth a binding credo."[15]

There is an inconsistency in the denial of absolutes. From a philosophical point of view it is self-defeating. This is manifest in the writing of Joseph Fletcher, one of the signatories of "Humanist Manifesto II." In his *Situation Ethics*, Fletcher declares, "The situationist avoids words like 'never' and 'perfect' and 'always' and 'complete' as he avoids the plague, as he avoids 'absolutely.' "[16] What Fletcher is in effect saying is: (1) "one should never use the word *never*"; (2) "one should always avoid using the word *always*"; (3) "one should absolutely deny all 'absolutes.' "

Certainly the relativist is not going to be content to deny only *some* divine absolutes. Both the wording and fervor of his denials indicate clearly that it is *all* absolutes he has in mind. For if it is only some divine absolutes he wishes to deny, then he is really no longer a secular humanist. He is some kind of ethical theist who differs from other theists only in the number of absolutes he holds.

Not only are the secular humanists inconsistent in principle when they attempt to deny all moral absolutes, they also are inconsistent in *practice.* Fletcher violates his own rule against universal statements in the same book, saying, "*No* unwanted and unintended baby should *ever* be born."[17] He also says, "Love is the *only* norm," and, "The ruling norm of Christian decision is love: *nothing* else."[18] Even the humanist manifestos and declaration speak in absolutistic terms: "This world community *must* renounce the resort to violence and force as a method of solving international disputes." Again, "War is obsolete. So is the use of nuclear, biological, and chemical weapons. It is a *planetary imperative* to reduce the level of military expenditures and turn these savings to peaceful and people-oriented uses."[19] Later on we read, "World poverty *must* cease. Hence extreme dis-

15. Ibid., p. 13.
16. Joseph Fletcher, *Situation Ethics: The New Morality* (Philadelphia: Westminster, 1966), pp. 43–44.
17. Ibid., p. 39 (emphasis added).
18. Ibid., p. 69 (emphasis added).
19. "Humanist Manifesto II," p. 21 (emphasis added).

proportions in wealth, income, and economic growth should be reduced on a *worldwide* basis."[20]

Moreover, secular humanists worthy of the name conduct their lives in accord with an absolute ideal: unconditional commitment to *man.* That, indeed, is what makes them secular humanists. Ultimate commitment is, as Paul Tillich notes, the essence of religion. All men have an infinite or absolute passion for something, Tillich insists. For the secular humanists "commitment to all humankind is *the highest commitment* of which we are capable."[21]

Among the moral absolutes advocated by many secular humanists today are intelligence, freedom, and tolerance. From reading their writings one gets the distinct impression that in practice they really desire all men at all times and in all places to act intelligently, to promote freedom, and to be tolerant. Indeed, the "Secular Humanist Declaration" says explicitly, "We oppose *any* tyranny over the mind of man, *any* effort . . . to shackle free thought."[22] If secular humanists believe there are exceptions to these principles, they do not advertise them. It is obvious, then, from both the writings and actions of secular humanists that they do believe in some moral absolutes.

Philosophically, secular humanism is a house without a foundation. It claims to have knowledge of certain things but denies the foundation of that knowledge. It claims to be reasonable but fails to posit an ultimate Reason. It denies that anything exists beyond nature, but stands outside nature to make this claim. It presents the view that only matter (or what is reducible to it) exists independently, and yet implies that there is an independent basis for this idea.

Ethically, secular humanism denies all absolutes—absolutely. Both in theory and in practice secular humanism has built its castle in the air. It is a lever that would move the world but has nowhere to place its fulcrum.

One may legitimately inquire as to why so many "rational" people believe in a system that lacks rational foundations. In brief, the answer seems to be that even "rational" people do not always make the most rational decision when it comes to ultimate questions which involve

20. Ibid., p. 22 (emphasis added).
21. Ibid., p. 23 (emphasis added).
22. "Secular Humanist Declaration," p. 4 (emphasis added).

God. The brilliant and famous atheist, Friedrich Nietzsche, made a revealing comment in this connection: "If one were to *prove* this God of the Christians to us, we should be even less able to believe in him."[23]

23. Nietzsche, *Antichrist*, in *The Portable Nietzsche*, ed. and trans. Walter Kaufmann (New York: Viking, 1968), p. 627.

15

The Social Arrogance of Secular Humanism

Secular humanism is not only religiously inadequate and philosophically insufficient, it is often socially arrogant. It optimistically claims to be able to solve all of man's social problems. The authors of "Humanist Manifesto II" say, "No deity will save us; we must save ourselves."[1] This attitude of self-sufficiency sometimes turns to naiveté. The father of John Stuart Mill believed that "all would be gained if the whole population were taught to read."[2]

The False Assumptions of Secular Humanism

Even some humanists have severely criticized contemporary humanism's social arrogance, which has blinded many humanists to the fact that some of their presuppositions are destructive to society. In an excellent book entitled *The Arrogance of Humanism*, David Ehrenfeld lists six of these basic humanistic assumptions:

1. All problems are soluble by people.
2. Many problems are soluble by technology.
3. Problems not soluble by technology have social or political solutions.

1. "Humanist Manifesto II," in *Humanist Manifestos I & II*, ed. Paul Kurtz (Buffalo: Prometheus, 1973), p. 16.
2. T. M. Kitwood, *What Is Human?* (Downers Grove, Ill.: Inter-Varsity, 1970), p. 50.

4. When the chips are down, man will find a solution before it is too late.
5. Some resources are infinite; all finite resources have substitutes.
6. Human civilization will survive.

These assumptions, says Ehrenfeld, are common to humanists of both the Left and the Right. Several other assumptions characterize humanists of the Left:

1. The truth will prevail.
2. Persecution defeats itself.
3. Man is naturally good and is corrupted only by his environment.
4. The world is immensely rich and is suffering chiefly from maldistribution.
5. It can be arranged that all unpleasant kinds of work be done by machines.[3]

These presuppositions are, of course, unprovable in an absolute sense. But, Ehrenfeld states, "as with all optimistic assumptions, it should take less evidence to discredit them than to lend them credence."[4] Unfortunately, "humanism, which proclaims and celebrates critical intelligence of humanity, has in the last analysis failed to invoke it where it is needed most, to test humanism's own faith."[5]

Further, humanists often speak contradictorily. Many, for example, believe in man's infinite possibilities, yet insist that we recognize man's limitations. Humanism, then, seems to be paradoxical: it negates what it affirms; it assumes what it cannot prove; it promises what it cannot produce.

There are, of course, other inconsistencies in the humanists' beliefs. For example, they have an unwavering faith in technology, yet they long to return to nature, which technology is destroying.

The Myths of Humanism

Like all religious people humanists have a set of beliefs they regard as factual. But many of these beliefs are no more than myths. They

3. David Ehrenfeld, *The Arrogance of Humanism* (New York: Oxford University Press, 1978), pp. 16 – 17. Both the title and many of the ideas for this chapter are suggested by Ehrenfeld's insightful book.
4. Ibid., p. 18.
5. Ibid., p. 19.

may appear to the humanist mind to be accurate, yet they lack credibility when examined more closely.

One of the humanist myths, which may be labeled the myth concerning the mind, is that we will eventually learn to control human behavior, and that we will gain this control through a thorough study of each individual's mental development. For this reason humanists place great emphasis on testing. Such testing is already administered at birth (e.g., the Apgar Scale), and continues in the child's early months (e.g., the Cattell Development and Intelligence Scale), in pre-school years (e.g., the Minnesota Preschool Scale), and in adulthood (e.g., the Minnesota Multiphasic Personality Inventory). One of the remarkable features of these tests is the vast amount of information that can be learned about an individual in a very short time. Indeed, an experienced tester can acquire this information without ever having seen the person. Humanists expect that by using this skill of testing to gain information about a person's "psychohistory" (that is, his mental development and condition), they will be able to predict that person's behavior and thus control it more completely.

In addition to the myth concerning the mind there is what may be called the myth concerning the body. Humanists believe it is inevitable we will learn to control our physical inheritance and destiny. They hope that this control will liberate us from most, if not all, of our physical ills and "help us approach the perfection that was once attributed only to machines and the gods themselves."[7]

This myth that man can control his body found literary expression in H. G. Wells's *Food of the Gods*, a novel about the discovery of a synthetic food that could make ordinary humans grow into giants.[8] Their physical stature was then assumed to be a sign of superiority in every other respect. More recently, characters that many of us have seen on television, superhuman Mr. Spock of "Star Trek" and Colonel Steve Austin of "The Six Million Dollar Man," personify the physical perfection that the humanists envision.

Meanwhile in the real world scientists strive to realize this myth. Several breakthroughs have encouraged them. For example, the cloning of a frog by a British scientist has encouraged the belief that it is possible to produce carbon-copy human beings. Furthermore,

---

6. The analysis in this section follows that of Ehrenfeld, *Arrogance*, pp. 27 – 46.

7. Ibid., p. 37.

8. See H. G. Wells, *The Food of the Gods* (London: Collins, 1966), pp. 21 – 30.

because scientists do have the ability to transfer genes from one organism to another, they believe that through genetic engineering they will be able to remove man's physical defects.

A third myth, the myth concerning the environment, is demonstrated by Herman Kahn and Anthony Wiener in their book *The Year 2000*. They have predicted one hundred technical innovations which they believe will be implemented in the last third of this century. Among them are several which deal with man's environment:

1. New techniques for preserving or improving the environment.
2. New and useful plant and animal species.
3. Widespread use of nuclear reactors for power.
4. Some control of weather and/or climate.
5. Design and extensive use of responsive and supercontrolled environments for private and public use.
6. Permanent manned satellites and lunar installations—interplanetary travel.
7. Application of space life systems or similar techniques to terrestrial installations.
8. Permanent inhabited undersea installations and perhaps even colonies.
9. Extensive genetic control for plants and animals.[9]

Even more far-reaching (and far-fetched) is the statement of futurologist Adrian Berry in his book *The Next Ten Thousand Years:* "There is no limit to growth, and there is no limit to what the developed nations can accomplish."[10]

Man will overcome his immediate environmental problems by widening his horizons to the whole universe. This cosmic optimism constitutes the humanistic myth concerning the environment. How is all of this to be accomplished? Technology. "Humanist Manifesto II" confidently proclaims,

> Using technology wisely, we can control our environment, conquer poverty, markedly reduce disease, extend our life-span, significantly

9. See Herman Kahn and Anthony Wiener, *The Year 2000: A Framework for Speculation on the Next Thirty-three Years* (New York: Macmillan, 1967), pp. 51 – 55, for this list of innovations.

10. Adrian Berry, *The Next Ten Thousand Years: A Vision of Man's Future in the Universe* (New York: Dutton, 1974), p. 39.

modify our behavior, alter the course of human evolution and cultural development, unlock vast new powers, and provide humankind with unparalleled opportunity for achieving an abundant and meaningful life.[11]

Some humanists believe that at last our destiny is in our own hands. Technology has provided unlimited power by which we can control our own environment.

The Falsity of Humanism's Myths

There is a stark contrast between the myths of humanism and reality. Ehrenfeld levels a devastating attack on these humanistic beliefs:

> The major reason for the prevalence of [expressions like] *hopefully = let us hope* is that deep within ourselves we know that our omnipotence is a sham, our knowledge and control of the future is weak and limited, our inventions and discoveries work, if they work at all, in ways that we do not expect, our planning is meaningless, our systems are running amok—in short, that the humanistic assumptions upon which our societies are grounded lack validity.[12]

He adds, "Evidence is piled all around us that the religion of humanity is self-destructive and foolish, yet the more it fails the more arrogant and preposterous are the claims of its priests." He also censures the overly optimistic forecasts of the humanists as a "wretched assortment of lies and delusions."[13]

The Failure of Testing

Ehrenfeld poses a crucial question: "With all this passion for testing, screening, placement, and correction, why are scholarship and intellectual achievement no better than they are?"[14] And why are the results of modern education so insignificant? Moreover, there are many potentially harmful effects which may result from testing chil-

11. "Humanist Manifesto II," p. 14.
12. Ehrenfeld, *Arrogance*, p. 58.
13. Ibid., p. 59.
14. Ibid., p. 75.

dren. Consider, for example, that a child labeled "minimally brain-damaged" (or worse) at an early age may be stigmatized until death.[15]

The Impossibility of Knowing All the Factors

Humanists assume without warrant that we will someday know enough about a sufficient number of human factors to make accurate prediction and control of human behavior possible. This causes one to reflect on Eric Kraus's warning about simplified model systems, and about the tripartite absurdity of long-range predictions:

1. We cannot know and gather in advance all the information that will be relevant.
2. We cannot know in advance what questions to ask of it.
3. Even if we did know this, we still could not make errorless deductions from what we know.

If it is practically impossible to make the expected humanistic improvements by collecting data and making projections, why are humanists so bent on doing so? For they repeatedly make predictions about matters which are in fact unpredictable and claim to know what is unknowable. Where does such arrogance come from? As C. S. Lewis noted, it apparently arises out of the same motivation behind magic—the desire for power over nature.[16]

The Inability to Change Human Behavior

B. F. Skinner's belief that one can effect behavior modification is well known (see chap. 2). The Skinnerians take it as a fact that there is an effective science of controlling human behavior. Skinner states his view clearly in *Walden Two*:

> "Mr. Castle," said Frazier very earnestly, "let me ask you a question. I warn you it will be the most terrifying question of your life. *What would you do if you found yourself in possession of an effective science*

---

15. Ibid., pp. 74 – 75.
16. C. S. Lewis, *The Abolition of Man* (New York: Macmillan, 1947), pp. 87 – 88.

of behavior? Suppose you suddenly found it possible to control the behavior of men as you wished. . . ."
"That's an assumption?"
"Take it as one if you like. *I* take it as a fact."[17]

This is not science, however, but a belief in magic. Skinner's thinking has been incisively criticized by Noam Chomsky:

> The question of evidence is beside the point, since the claims dissolve into triviality or incoherence under analysis. Claims with regard to the inevitability of future discoveries are more ambiguous. Is Skinner saying that as a matter of necessity, science will show that behavior is completely determined by the environment? If so, his claim can be dismissed as pure dogmatism, foreign to the "nature of scientific inquiry."[18]

Oddly enough two Skinnerians, Keller and Marian Breland, proved the invalidity of Skinnery's theory. Their aim was to see if their conditioning of animals would hold up outside the laboratory. They conditioned over six thousand animals, including everything from raccoons to reindeer. But their failures to change animal behavior were unexpectedly frequent. A raccoon, which had been conditioned to deposit coins in a piggy bank to obtain food, when outside the laboratory not only would not let go of the coins, but spent seconds, even minutes, rubbing them together. (It is well known that raccoons rub and wash their food before eating it.) The natural habits of the raccoon made the experiment to modify its behavior unfeasible. Similar failures were recorded with chickens and pigs, whose natural behavior repeatedly interfered with attempts to recondition them.

The fallacy in these experiments was the assumption that animals are a *tabula rasa* (blank slate) prior to conditioning. This constitutes a denial of the biological reality that every organism has inherent characteristics that will resist the most scientific (or unscientific) attempts to change it.[19]

---

17. B. F. Skinner, *Walden Two* (New York: Macmillan, 1948), p. 240.
18. Noam Chomsky, *For Reasons of State* (New York: Vintage, 1973), p. 321.
19. Ehrenfeld, *Arrogance*, pp. 79 – 80.

Even more preposterous than attempts to change animal behavior is the humanist assumption that human behavior can be engineered. Ehrenfeld appropriately asks at this point, "How can we possibly expect that a 'behavioral engineering' incapable of making a pig let go of a piece of wood or a chicken refrain from pecking at a ball, can neatly excise the competitive spirit from an otherwise intact humanity?"[20]

The Inability to Improve Man's Physical Nature

The arrogance of humanism extends as well to the body. Although H. G. Wells's story of a food that can make man bigger and better in every way is pure science fiction, it does reflect a profound dissatisfaction with our bodies. But even if we could make Johnny two times bigger, there is not a shred of scientific evidence to show that this would make him two times better!

Despite the lauding of the bionic man, "the cold truth is that our bionic devices and spare parts can never be the equal of the organs they are meant to replace."[21] Eyeglasses, for example, have been perfected for centuries, and yet they are incomparably inferior to a good pair of eyes. One sees better with glasses, but he experiences discomfort and inconvenience. Something is always lost when one must resort to a mechanical device. To expect that bionic devices will result in net gain is to believe in magic.

The Failure to Conquer Disease

Most of us are grateful for antibiotics. But their blessing is mixed. Some patients have died upon injection with antibiotics. Then too there is the proliferation of antibiotic-resistant bacteria. Nearly all major diseases have developed strains highly resistant to antibiotics. This has committed us to a feverish race in which we must come up with new antibiotics faster than the bacteria can develop resistance!

Tranquilizers are helpful in treating some mental diseases. But they are also used in ways that may be undesirable. For example, they are widely used to cope with the tensions of modern life. This,

20. Ibid., p. 81.
21. Ibid., p. 85.

says Ehrenfeld, is "like wearing ear plugs to bed so as not to be disturbed by the noise of the fire alarm."[22]

Nowhere is man's self-deception so marked as in the war against cancer. After decades of research and billions of dollars what has been achieved? "A handful of mostly minor cancers can now be arrested or reversed, and a very few can be eliminated entirely."[23] But even the means of treatment can themselves cause cancer, and the rate of cure for most cancers of the breast, digestive tract, and lungs is about the same as a quarter of a century ago. What is most embarrassing to the technological humanists is that perhaps the very urban and industrial centers they have created have greatly increased the cancer rate and now account for up to 80 or 90 percent of all cancer! Is it possible that the technological cure is worse than the natural disease?

The ability to prolong life is a credit to modern medical "advance." But even here there is an unfortunate irony. While we have discovered medical ways of prolonging life we have not found out how to enjoy these added years. It is ironic that "the society that discovers the ways of curing seems incapable of creating an environment in which the cures can be enjoyed."[24] We have come to equate life with the mere avoidance of death. But in fact we have lost the true value of life in our quest to avoid death. Elderly people whose lives have been extended often live them out in impersonal institutions or in dependence on machines rather than in the personal context of the family. We have lost the personal pleasure of the human family in our "humanistic" quest to gain longevity.

In view of the notorious failure of secular humanism to achieve social well-being, Ehrenfeld offers two "laws" based on the experience of the last few centuries:

1. Most scientific discoveries and technological inventions can be developed in such a way that they are capable of doing great damage to human beings, their cultures, and their environments.
2. If a discovery or a technology can be used for evil purposes, it will be so used.[25]

22. Ibid., p. 89.
23. Ibid., p. 90.
24. Ibid., p. 93.
25. Ibid., p. 97.

In connection with these laws it should be mentioned that the irreversibility of some of our actions, which is often ignored, is cause for persistent fear.

The Failure of Machines

The myth of the machine has been a persistent one among humanists despite its notable failures. True, machines have placed men on the moon and replaced them on assembly lines. And computers have sped up complex calculation processes a hundredfold. But have machines brought about the desired humanist millennium?

The first use of the word *robot* occurred in a Czech play, *R. U. R.*, written by Karel Čapek in 1920. In it one of the characters portends, "You see, so many Robots are being manufactured that people are becoming superfluous; man is really a survival."[26] No doubt Čapek would have been horrified to discover that many have taken the idea seriously.

The humanistic hope in the machine has developed into what almost amounts to worship. Thus any "machine malfunction" or "computer breakdown" is blamed not on the machine but on human error—men made the machines and programmed the computers. It is ironic, then, that the humanistic faith in man's own divinity continues to exist. Indeed, "if we are gods, . . . and if we have created the machines, why do we find ourselves in this position of inferiority vis-à-vis our own creation?"[27] Is the creature greater than the creator? One explanation may be the age-old tendency of man to worship the product of his own hands. It is also true that no religion can survive if it will not affirm its own miracles. Perhaps we must worship the machine if we wish to maintain the myth that technology can work miracles.

But machines are not easy to worship. There is no personality or final purpose in them. They can turn unpredictably on any purpose in whose name they are invoked. They are subject to continual breakdown.

One final irony plagues the humanist. His technology has produced the neutron bomb, which destroys people but leaves their

26. Quoted in Ehrenfeld, *Arrogance*, p. 100.
27. Ibid., p. 101.

machines intact! Surely it is the ultimate irony that our machine could ultimately destroy us. Let us hope we heed the saying, "Let not the H-bomb be the sequel in which all men are cremated equal."

The Inability to Manage Man's Environment

One of the most spectacular failures of human control is manifested in our dealings with human environments. In no important instance have we been able to demonstrate complete successful control of our world. In fact, we do not even understand it well enough to be able to manage it in theory. For example, the so-called protective treatment given the stained-glass windows of Chartres Cathedral not only resulted in an unpleasantly glossy look, it effectively resisted its own removal. Even the heralded solar pump, which can raise water inexpensively for the Arizona desert, will create new difficulties. Among the results of the solar pump will be a lowering of the water table, the drying up of existing wells and springs, and contamination of underground water with agricultural chemicals.

Not only are these humanistic "solutions" only quasi-solutions at best, they also dramatize what Eugene Schwartz called "overskill" in his book by that title. Overskill is "the dialectical process whereby a solution to one problem generates sets of new problems that eventually preclude solutions."[28] He outlines five steps in this process:

1. Because of the interrelationships and limitations existing within a closed system, a techno-social solution is never complete and hence is a quasi-solution.
2. Each quasi-solution generates a residue of new techno-social problems arising from: (a) incompleteness, (b) augmentation, and (c) secondary effects.
3. The new problems proliferate at a faster rate than solutions can be found to meet them.
4. Each successive set of residue problems is more difficult to solve than predecessor problems because of seven factors: (a) dynamics of technology, (b) increased complexity, (c) increased cost, (d) decreased resources, (e) growth and expansion, (f) requirements for greater control, and (g) inertia of social institutions.

28. Ibid., p. 107.

5. The residue of unsolved techno-social problems converge in an advanced technological society to a point where techno-social solutions are no longer possible.[29]

As to the delusion of our space age that we can find a solution to problems here by leaving mother earth, Ehrenfeld says,

> This is an immature and irresponsible idea, that having fouled this world with our inventions, we will somehow do better in other orbits. However, if one sees humanism for what it is, a religion without God, then the idea is not so strange: space with its space stations and space inhabitants is just a replacement for heaven with its angels.[30]

Space is little more than a watered-down heaven for modern humanist believers. However, they fail to realize the immense difficulties of living in space. If the space station is not under control at all times, the inhabitants will die. One blackout such as happened in New York City on July 13 and 14, 1977, would wipe out the space colony. It is also forgotten by these would-be space "pilgrims" that a space station will be far different from earth. For the life-support systems of earth are vast, complex, and self-regulating, and have been entirely successful for uninterrupted millennia. All artificial life-support systems are machines, and sooner or later all machines fail. Perhaps most of the space enthusiasts have never been serious gardeners. If they had been, they would not be so optimistic about the future of life in barren space, where earth and nature will not be available to correct their mistakes.

One humanist frankly confesses man's inability to control the environment:

> We have been reading the old biblical story of the expulsion from the Garden of Eden too carelessly of late; like fundamentalists, we must pay more attention to detail. For was not the Garden of Eden described as a *better* place than the world outside after the fall? And was it not the clear implication of Genesis that all the new-found skills and knowledge that the fateful apple could provide were imperfect? The serpent was lying when he said, "Ye shall be as gods."[31]

29. See Eugene Schwartz, *Overskill* (New York: Ballantine, 1971), for a development of these ideas.

30. Ehrenfeld, *Arrogance*, p. 120.

31. Ibid., pp. 124–125.

The Failure to Recognize Human Limitations

There are four basic limitations of man which humanism fails to recognize. First, there are the limits imposed by our inability to know the future, and thus to make accurate long-range predictions. Second, there are limits imposed by the consequences of prior failures, which were based on the false assumptions that we could control the environment. Third, there is the limit that is described by the maximization theory of John von Neumann and Oskar Morgenstern, which says in effect that in a complex world we cannot work everything out for the best simultaneously. Fourth, there is the limit inherent in the uncertainty principle. This is the idea that our ability to seek technical solutions to certain kinds of problems grows along with our capacity to augment and multiply these kinds of problems. In view of these limitations it is difficult to understand the boundless optimism of humanism.

Even though sober-minded scientists were writing books on the limitations of science, as early as 1933,[32] in that very year secular humanists collectively pronounced their unbounded optimism for the future. "Man is at last becoming aware that he is alone responsible for the realization of the world of his dreams, that he has within himself the power for its achievement."[33]

Forty years and another world war later even humanists had to admit that this "earlier statement seem[s] far too optimistic."[34] This notwithstanding, humanist optimism in man's unbounded ability still reigns. The recent "Secular Humanist Declaration" is an example of this optimism:

> We believe the scientific method, though imperfect, is still the most reliable way of understanding the world. Hence, we look to the natural, biological, social, and behavioral sciences for knowledge of the universe and man's place within it. Modern astronomy and physics have opened up exciting new dimensions of the universe: they have enabled humankind to explore the universe by means of space travel. Biology and the social and behavioral sciences have expanded our understanding of human behavior.[35]

32. See, for example, J. W. N. Sullivan, *The Limitations of Science* (1933; repr. ed., New York: Mentor, 1949).

33. "Humanist Manifesto I," p. 10.

34. "Humanist Manifest II," p. 13.

35. "A Secular Humanist Declaration," in *Free Inquiry*, Winter 1980–81, pp. 5–6.

The Inability of Reason Alone to Produce a Better World

Rational humanist Salvador Luria offers justification for genetic recombination studies:

> To cope with the stresses and pressures that our own species will have to face in the next couple of centuries and to create a world fit for the new billions of human beings to live in, we shall have to understand as precisely as possible all interactions within our own body cells.[36]

In this statement there are at least three unproven assumptions which are typical of secular humanism. First, there is the assumption that by our reason we can create a world fit for future generations. This is certainly challengeable in view of the fact we have taken a world perfectly fit for human dwelling and turned it into one which is chemically polluted, politically tumultuous, and socially inhumane. Second, there is the unfounded assumption that man's reason can achieve such a high degree of perception that he will be able to understand all the interactions within our body's cells. Third, there is the enigmatic assumption that this improbable understanding will help us to make the world fit to live in.[37] To these assumptions a fourth may be added. Humanists assume that man's reason alone can point the path to justice and that humanity can be induced to follow it. Such is the unbridled optimism of secular humanism.

Secular humanists also offer the hope that "artificial intelligence" may be able to solve our greatest problems. They expect computers to surpass many functions of normal intelligence. Here again man is not only overcomplimenting himself on the ability to create, but he vainly expects water to rise higher than its source, or the effect to be greater than its cause.

Hubert Dreyfus has written a critique of artificial intelligence in a book entitled *What Computers Can't Do*. He notes that in each case of computer success there has been a pattern of initial success followed by failure. The overprojection based on early success has been called "the fallacy of the successful first step." In the case of language

36. Salvador Luria, "The Goals of Science," *Bulletin of the Atomic Scientists* 5, no. 33 (May 1977), p. 313.

37. See Hubert L. Dreyfus, *What Computers Can't Do: A Critique of Artificial Reason* (New York: Harper & Row, 1972), pp. 197 – 217.

translation, for example, after certain crude successes there have been no real breakthroughs, nor are any expected. For translation demands more than a mechanical dictionary and the laws of grammar. The order of words in a sentence does not in itself convey the author's meaning. The grammar alone, including the surrounding context, does not always indicate which of several possible meanings the author had in mind.[38]

The basic assumption behind the optimism of some workers in the field of artificial intelligence is that human and mechanical information-processing ultimately involve the same operations. This in turn rests upon four assumptions. First, there is the biological assumption that the brain works like a computer, by means of on/off switches. Second, there is the psychological assumption that the mind can be viewed as a device which operates on bits of information according to formal rules. Third, there is the epistemological assumption that all knowledge can be formalized and expressed in terms of logical relations. Fourth, there is the ontological assumption that all important facts about the world can be abstracted, stored, and used independently of their original context, that they are "situation-free" and "logically independent."

Needless to say, there is no compelling reason to accept any of these assumptions, and all of them may be false. Indeed, it is safe to say that computers are not really intelligent in any human sense at all. They can do only what they are told to do and no more. They are mechanical slaves. Why the master should worship the slave he has created is indeed a mystery.

There is an unfounded arrogance about the social expectations of secular humanists. They promise a manmade millennium but so far have not even produced a local paradise. They promise heaven on earth but have not even delivered man from his earthly hell. They have unlimited trust in man's severely limited reason.

38. See the discussion in Ehrenfeld, *Arrogance*, pp. 150 – 151.

Bibliography

Expositions of Various Kinds of Secular Humanism

Dewey, John. *A Common Faith*. New Haven, Conn.: Yale University, 1934.

Freud, Sigmund. *The Future of an Illusion*. New York: Doubleday, 1957.

Fromm, Erich. *Man for Himself.* New York: Premier, 1968.

_____. *Marx's Concept of Man*. New York: Frederick Ungar, 1961.

"Humanist Manifestos I & II." Edited by Paul Kurtz. Buffalo: Prometheus, 1973.

Huxley, Julian. *Religion Without Revelation*. New York: Mentor, 1957.

Kolenda, Konstantin. *Religion Without God*. Buffalo, Prometheus, 1976.

Kurtz, Paul, ed. *The Humanist Alternative*. London: Pemberton, 1973.

Lamont, Corliss. *The Philosophy of Humanism*. 5th ed., revised and enlarged. New York: Philosophical Library, 1949.

Marx, Karl, and Engels, Friedrich. *Manifesto of the Communist Party*. Moscow: Progress Publishers, 1977.

_____. *On Religion*. New York: Schocken, 1964.

Rand, Ayn. *For the New Intellectual*. New York: Signet, 1961.

Sartre, Jean-Paul. *Existentialism and Humanism*. Translated by Philip Mairet. London: Methuen, 1948.

"A Secular Humanist Declaration." In *Free Inquiry*, Winter 1980 – 81.

Skinner, B. F. *Beyond Freedom and Dignity*. New York: Bantam, 1971.

Storer, Morris B., ed. *Humanist Ethics*. Buffalo, Prometheus, 1980.

Expositions of Various Kinds of Christian Humanism

Allen, Edgar L. *Christian Humanism: A Guide to the Thought of Jacques Maritain*. London: Hodder & Stoughton, 1950.

Barcus, Nancy B. *Developing a Christian Mind.* Downers Grove, Ill.: Inter-Varsity, 1977.

Breen, Quirinus. *Christianity and Humanism.* Grand Rapids: Eerdmans, 1968.

Kilby, Clyde S. *Christianity and Aesthetics.* Downers Grove, Ill.: Inter-Varsity, 1961.

Kitwood, T. M. *What Is Human?* Downers Grove, Ill.: Inter-Varsity, 1970.

Lewis, C. S. *Studies in Medieval and Renaissance Literature.* New York: Cambridge University, 1966.

Maritain, Jacques. *Integral Humanism: Temporal and Spiritual Problems of a New Humanism.* South Bend, Ind.: University of Notre Dame, 1973.

————. *True Humanism.* Westport, Conn.: Greenwood, 1970.

Molnar, Thomas. *Christian Humanism.* Chicago: Franciscan Herald, 1978.

Niebuhr, H. Richard. *Christ and Culture.* New York: Harper, 1956.

Sayers, Dorothy Leigh. "Toward a Christian Esthetic." In *The Whimsical Christian.* New York: Macmillan, 1978.

Shaw, Joseph M., et al., eds. *Readings in Christian Humanism.* Minneapolis: Augsburg, 1982.

Strawson, William. *The Christian Approach to the Humanist.* London: Lutterworth, 1970.

Evaluations of Secular Humanism

Blackham, Harold J., ed. *Objections to Humanism.* Westport, Conn.: Greenwood, 1974.

Clark, Gordon H. *Behaviorism and Christianity.* Jefferson, Md.: The Trinity Foundation, 1982.

Conn, Harry. *Four Trojan Horses of Humanism.* Milford, Mich.: Mott Media, 1982.

Cosgrove, Mark P. *The Essence of Human Nature.* Grand Rapids: Zondervan, 1977.

————. *Psychology Gone Awry.* Grand Rapids: Zondervan, 1979.

Duncan, Homer. *Secular Humanism: The Most Dangerous Religion in America.* Lubbock, Tex.: Missionary Crusader, 1979.

Ehrenfeld, David. *The Arrogance of Humanism.* New York: Oxford University, 1978.

Geisler, Norman L. *Ethics: Alternatives and Issues.* Grand Rapids: Zondervan, 1971.

Geisler, Norman L; Brooke, Al; and Keough, Mark. *The Creator in the Courtroom: "Scopes II."* Milford, Mich.: Mott Media, 1982.

Guinness, Os. *The Dust of Death.* Downers Grove, Ill.: Inter-Varsity, 1973.

LaHaye, Tim. *The Battle for the Mind.* New York: Revell, 1980.

Lewis, C. S. *The Abolition of Man.* New York: Macmillan, 1947.

_____. *God in the Dock: Essays on Theology and Ethics.* Edited by Walter Hooper. Grand Rapids: Eerdmans, 1970.

Lutzer, Erwin. *The Necessity of Ethical Absolutes.* Grand Rapids: Zondervan, 1981.

McDonald, H. D. *The Christian View of Man.* Foundations for Faith. Westchester, Ill.: Good News, 1981.

MacKay, Donald M. *Human Science and Human Dignity.* Downers Grove, Ill.: Inter-Varsity, 1979.

Packer, J. I. *Knowing Man.* Westchester, Ill.: Good News, 1979.

Phillips, J. B. *God Our Contemporary.* New York: Macmillan, 1960.

Schaeffer, Francis A. *A Christian Manifesto.* Westchester, Ill.: Good News, 1981.

_____. *Back to Freedom and Dignity.* Downers Grove, Ill.: Inter-Varsity, 1972.

_____. *Whatever Happened to the Human Race?* Old Tappan, N.J.: Revell, 1979.

Webber, Robert E. *Secular Humanism: Threat and Challenge.* Grand Rapids: Zondervan, 1982.

Whitehead, John W. *The Second American Revolution.* Elgin, Ill.: David C. Cook, 1982.

_____. *The Separation Illusion.* Milford, Mich.: Mott Media, 1980.

Wilder-Smith, A. E. *Man's Origin, Man's Destiny: A Critical Survey of the Principles of Evolution and Christianity.* Minneapolis: Bethany Fellowship, 1968.